Books are to be returned on or before
the last date below.

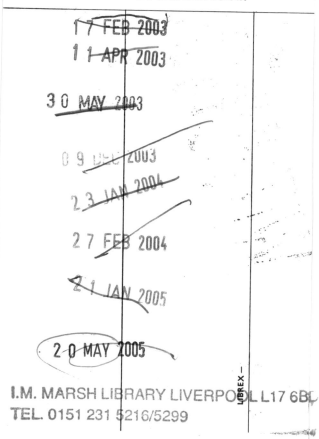

Dalesman Publishing Company
Stable Courtyard, Broughton Hall,
Skipton, North Yorkshire BD23 3AE


First published as Safety on the Hills 1995
Reprinted in this format 1997

Text © Kevin Walker 1997
Cover by Graham Thompson
Illustrations by Jeremy Ashcroft/Harry Sailisbury

Printed by Amadeus Press, Huddersfield

A British Library Cataloguing in Publication
record is available for this book

ISBN 185568 112 9

# Contents

Useful addresses:

British Mountaineering Council
177-179 Burton Road, West Didsbury,
Manchester M20 2BB
Tel 0161 4454747 Fax 0161 4454500

Kevin Walker Mountain Activities
74 Beacons Park, Brecon, Powys LD3 9BQ
Tel/Fax 01874-625111

Mountain Leader Training Board
Address & telephone as BMC

The Ramblers' Association
1-5 Wandsworth Road, London SW8 2LJ
Tel 0171-582-6826

Scottish Sports Council
Caledonia House, South Gyle, Edinburgh EH12 9DQ
Tel 0131-317-7200

# Introduction

When I first started instructing mountain activities, almost 20 years ago as I write this, I used to tell my clients that keeping safe in the mountains was purely a matter of common sense – nothing more, nothing less. I used to reason that if one was sensible and took no unnecessary risks, all would be fine.

I was wrong! With hindsight, I have modified and developed my ideas to the extent that I now consider mountain safety to be far more complex. The major problem is that it is impossible to use your common sense if you do not recognise the risk or appreciate the dangers. No-one but an idiot deliberately puts himself into a life threatening situation, yet year after year people are killed and injured on the hills. I guess the vast majority of these mountain accidents are caused, not by stupidity, but by ignorance – the people involved neither understood nor appreciated the total risk involved in what they were doing.

Going into the mountains for the first time is a little like a young child playing with a box of matches: the pieces of wood are great toys until one is struck accidentally. Even when the child puts his finger in the flame and realises that this hurts, he has still not experienced the complete risk – it is not until the flames start spreading to clothing or furnishings that the major risk becomes apparent, and by then it is probably too late. Of course, an element of risk is an important part of the adventure and enjoyment of the mountains, and this holds equally true whether you visit the hills to climb, scramble or simply to walk. Without an element of risk, the adventure would be reduced to the commonplace and the experience made less worthwhile. So the risk is essential – but so is the assessment of that risk, and to my mind one of the most enjoyable aspects of the art of mountaincraft is solving the puzzle of how to stay safe, of striking a balance between danger and safety.

One of the most significant aspects of solving the puzzle is that every situation you meet will be unique. Despite common threads (most of them to do with a lack of awareness of potential hazards!), no two mountain accidents have ever been caused by exactly the same set of circumstances. Similarly, no two days on the hill can ever be exactly the same, simply because there is an almost infinite number of interrelated variables at work every time you go out. You could sit on precisely the same stone at the same time of day facing the same direction, every day for a year, and you would see 365 different views.

If you have picked up this book in the hope that it encapsulates mountain safety you will be disappointed, for that would be an impossible task. In any case, this is not so much a book about how to avoid risks as a book concerned with the appreciation and assessment of risks, and there is a subtle but significant difference. I have attempted to give mountaincraft a framework, some form of shape, giving you some hooks on which to hang your thoughts and a structure which you can clothe with your experiences. I hope it will open up a greater understanding and awareness of the mountain environment, and of the myriad facets which make up the mountain experience.

If you are new to the pleasures of the mountains, you should not expect this book to tell you everything you need to know in order to keep safe! Mountaincraft is an art, so it is impossible to become proficient simply by reading a book. As with any art you can only learn the skills through practical experience in a range of geographical areas and weather conditions. Although the basic techniques themselves are fairly simple, a basic requirement is that of judging when to use which skills and techniques and in what combination. This means that even if you are a skilled navigator, a proficient climber, and a capable weather-forecaster, you will still need to exercise your judgement if you want to stay safe. Good judgement is essential, but even the most experienced mountaineers get it wrong, so you should be aware that you can make mistakes, be ready to admit to them, and be open-minded enough to alter your plans accordingly and learn from the mistakes.

Most importantly, I hope this book gets you thinking and stimulates arguments and conversations. If there's something you vehemently disagree with, please write and tell me! None of us is foolproof – in the mountains there is no such thing as an expert – and I firmly believe that the interchange of ideas between mountain enthusiasts is extremely valuable.

## Acknowledgements

This book would not have been possible without the assistance of the countless people with whom I have shared time on the hill. In particular I would like to thank Geoff Arkless, Bob Barrington, Chris Hurley,

Steve Pedrazzoli and Ian Waddington for countless hours of fine mountain experience and discussion. I am also indebted to everyone at Crickhowell Adventure Gear for allowing me to play with bits of equipment and generally get in the way. Thanks, too, to Les for putting up with me as the deadline loomed closer, to Megan for persuading me that the book was not the most important thing in life, to Guy and Paul for showing me that my word processor had some in-built games, and to the gang at the George and the RAFA for providing diversion, understanding, great company and alcohol!

## How to use this book

What with new materials, synthetic fibres and computer design, things change so very quickly nowadays. Whereas in the past you only had to choose between one or two items when selecting new gear, you are now faced with a plethora of items, some of which are next to useless but most of which are excellent. Perhaps because of this, it seems to me that many newcomers to mountain activities have only a passing understanding of the basic principles, and it was with this in mind that I decided to write this book. Because I am dealing with basics, I have deliberately steered away from mentioning specific models, trade names, etc.

Although modern equipment and clothing have done much to aid the safe enjoyment of the mountains, they have also created their own dangers. It is, for example, very easy to be lulled into a false sense of security when you cannot feel how bad the weather is; similarly , there is a danger that you may become over-confident because you are using the very latest in ice axe and crampon technology. Good equipment is not a substitute for good technique. Buying the latest piece of kit will not make up for a lack of basic experience, nor will it provide an excuse for unsound practice.

I have divided the book into eleven sections. Although such division may seem somewhat arbitrary, I believe that the topics covered within each section sit well together, and I hope this makes the book easier to consult. Key words appear in bold, and I have cross referenced information where I have felt this was appropriate. I have deliberately steered away from detailing certain skills which I felt could only be learned through practical experience. Technical rock climbing and many of the winter skills (notably step cutting and crampon technique) fall into this category, as do the skills of outdoor first aid, and if you wish to pursue these activities I would encourage you to learn from a more exper-ienced companion or attend a course run by a suitably qualified instructor. If you wish to get more information about any given topic, there are suggestions for further reading at the back of the book, and a few addresses which I believe might be of use can be found on page 6.

Last but by no means least, this book is not a substitute for personal experience. Although there are topics covered within which may be useful if consulted when on the hill, the book should really live on a handy bookshelf where it can be consulted before you visit the mountains, rather than in the pocket of your rucksack.

# Basic do's and don'ts

### 1. Always take the basic minimum kit
In summer this should comprise sturdy boots, warm, windproof clothing, full set of waterproofs, woollen hat, gloves or mittens, map (1:50,000 scale as a minimum; 1:25,000 in more complex areas), suitable compass, whistle, survival bag, emergency rations, first aid kit, food and drink for the day, and a small rucksack (not a plastic carrier bag!).

If you intend to do any scrambling take a suitable rope and think carefully about wearing a helmet.

If you intend to camp in the wild you will also need a tent (or some other form of shelter), stove and pans, sleeping bag and sleepmat, extra dry clothing, lighting, and suitable rations.

In winter (including late autumn and early spring) you need extra items including a headtorch and spare batteries, spare warm clothing, overmitts and gaiters. If there is snow and ice around you will also need an ice axe, possibly a pair of crampons, and some ski goggles or snow glasses. At least one person in the party should carry a sleeping bag.

### 2. Let someone know where you are going
Unless you are going alone or are in charge of a group, this need not be anything too detailed, but should give at least a rough outline of your proposed route and when you expect to return.

### 3. Learn to use a map and compass effectively
Many mountain accidents are precipitated by poor navigation.

### 4. Get a local weather forecast
Mountains make their own weather and conditions can change alarmingly. Get a forecast for the local

area and, if new to the area, seek local advice.

### 5. Know the basic ABC of first aid
If something goes wrong you could be a long way from help in terms of both time and distance. It makes sense to know at least a little about first aid.

### 6. Be honest about your ability and expertise
Plan your routes according to your abilities and the expected conditions, and never be afraid to turn back. The more challenging routes will be more enjoyable when you have the skills to accomplish them.

### 7. Be aware of your surroundings
Keep your eyes on the weather, your companions, and other people. Be observant.

### 8. Take extra care during descent
The vast majority of mountain accidents happen during descent.

### 9. Be winter wise
Never venture onto snow clad hills without carrying an ice axe (and knowing how to use it).

### 10. Have some idea of emergency procedures
At the very least you should know how to call out a mountain rescue team, and you should also know something of the causes, treatment and avoidance of mountain hypothermia. It will also be of benefit if you have given prior thought to what you would do in the event of an emergency.

### 11. Respect the mountain environment
Be conservation minded not just to the physical environment but to the human environment as well. Take nothing but photographs; leave nothing but goodwill; disturb nothing but the air around you.

# 1 Clothing and footwear

Going to your local gear shop and buying the most expensive pair of boots and the latest in breathable-fabric technology jackets is not going to keep you safe on the hills, per se. These items do not possess any magic properties of their own – it is the how, when and why of their use that is important.

In this section we are going to look at various items of clothing and footwear – not individual models so much as broad types. As with most other aspects of mountain safety, what is important is that you understand the basic concepts – the logic behind the arguments – so that you are in a position to make an educated choice when you come to buy and use garments. To put it more succinctly, it is not what you wear which is important so much as the under-standing of why you wear it. Once you know the basics, you can visit your local friendly gear shop and ask all sorts of awkward questions. If the retailer cannot answer them (or cannot find the answer fairly quickly), then I suggest you are in the wrong shop!

One of the major problems is that there is no such thing as the ideal mountainwear. Not only will the most suitable clothing vary from person to person according to individual preference, but it will also vary from hour to hour as external conditions change. As you will see later in the book, not only do mountains make their own weather, they also tend to change it, often with surprising speed. Due to this the clothing that you wear or carry may have to protect you from a wide variety of weather conditions during the same trip. Obviously, this factor is even more pronounced if you are away from a valley base for two or more days whilst on an extended trip or expedition.

## The human machine

It will be helpful if you think of the body as a machine – a modern, high-tech model that requires precise operating conditions if it is to perform at optimum levels. There are two basic parts to this machine: the core (containing all the controlling mechanisms such as the vital organs), and the shell (all the external bits like skin and flesh and muscles). *See figure 1.* In order for this machine to operate efficiently, the temperature of the core must be maintained within very precise limits. If this core temperature falls (as hypothermia) or rises (as in heat stroke), even by only a small amount (i.e. +/- 1° Celsius), the efficiency of the brain and all the other vital organs will begin to deteriorate. The greater the fall or rise of core temperature, the greater the impairment.

Even if the core temperature is maintained to within its limits, it is possible that extremes of temperature at the shell will cause a number of problems, the most obvious being that of frostbite.

The main function of clothing, therefore, is to maintain the core temperature and to protect the shell, and particularly the extremities, from extremes of temperature. Due to the mountain environment experienced by most people, it is protection from cold and wet which is the most critical. A secondary, but no less significant function is to protect the shell from other aspects of the environment such as the danger from cuts, abrasions, etc.

In broad terms the human machine creates its own heat through stored energy – gained through food and fat reserves – and via muscular activity. It can also gain heat through external heat sources such as the sun. Heat loss can occur in any of five ways. In the mountain environment, these are often found in combination with one another.

Conduction is the mechanism whereby heat is transferred between two objects which are in contact with one another. For example, if you sit on a cold rock there will be a transfer of heat between your body and the rock. If the rock is hotter than you, it will warm you up, losing some of its heat as it does so. More commonly, the rock will be colder than you and you will therefore lose heat to the rock. In normal circumstances, your clothing will act as a barrier between you and the rock, thus preventing the heat loss

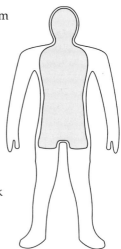

*Figure 1: The Human Machine. The shaded area represents the core; the remainder, the shell*

from becoming uncomfortable. However, this is not the case if your clothing is wet as water is a good conductor of heat. Indeed, if you are soaked to the skin, your wet clothing will conduct heat away from your body at about 250 times the rate of similar dry clothing. For our purposes, convection can be defined as the cooling effect of air passing over the body or through the clothing. Unless there is an effective barrier between the air and the skin (or between the wind and any insulating layers of clothing), there will be a noticeable heat loss. It is important to realise that the wind does not have to be strong for this to occur. Indeed, even a slight breeze can cause a marked heat loss.

Evaporation can be a major cause of heat loss in the mountain environment. To get an idea of the power of evaporation, wet a small section of the back of your hand and blow across it. Where you blow on dry skin, your breath will feel slightly warm; where you blow on wet skin, the area will feel suddenly colder. Of course, it is not just atmospheric moisture (i.e. mist, rain, snowmelt, etc.) which can dampen the clothing – body moisture in the form of sweat can also have an effect. Many people underestimate the importance of effective ventilation, especially on long ascents. Getting the ventilation right can take practice. You need to try and ventilate enough to prevent sweating without overdoing it so that you lose body heat through convection. You should also take into consideration that sweating is the body's natural response to overheating.

Radiation is the mechanism whereby heat is transferred from the source (i.e. the body) to the air, and its importance as a mechanism of heat loss is often underestimated. For example, even on those rare, still days when there is not a breath of wind, you could be losing up to 50% of the body's heat production if you are not wearing a hat. Within certain limits, it is fair to say that the colder the temperature or the stronger the wind, the greater the effect.

Last, but by no means least, we come to respiration. The very act of breathing will have a cooling effect as the moisture in the breath evaporates. Although this heat loss is not normally marked, the effect can be significant during strenuous ascents in cold weather, especially at altitude, and in cases where the person concerned is bordering on the hypothermic.

Although an understanding of the mechanisms is vital, it is equally essential to keep things in perspective for, in practice, it is very difficult to separate the five different functions. Indeed, they all tend to work hand in hand, each one affecting the other. In an attempt to make this more clear, let's use as an example a poorly clothed, inexperienced walker who has left his car and toiled up a steep slope to reach a viewpoint on a ridge – a common enough scenario in popular tourist areas.

The weather is not particularly bad at the roadside but it is colder on the tops, there is a noticeable (although not strong) breeze blowing, and the odd low cloud is scraping across the ridge making conditions occasionally moist and misty. On reaching the viewpoint, the walker is hot and sticky. Muscular effort has produced heat, and the lack of ventilation has resulted in sweat which has soaked the clothing nearest his skin. Atmospheric moisture (the mist droplets) has also penetrated his outer clothing, and the stronger currents of the breeze pass through all his clothing to reach his skin. As it was not cold at the car, he did not see the necessity to take either hat or gloves. He also underestimated the distance due to the foreshortening effect of looking uphill, and the exertion has left him breathless and tired. He has sat on a convenient rock to admire the view (which can occasionally be seen through the mist!).

The level of heat loss in this scenario is not only awesome, it is also potentially lethal! There will be a considerable amount of radiation from the walker's uncovered head, and significant conduction into the rock on which he is sitting. Further heat will be escaping due to his high rate of respiration. The fact that his clothing is damp from the outer layers right through to his skin means that there is marked heat loss through conduction, convection, and evaporation.

Moreover, the strength of the breeze is such that the stronger blasts of air pass through his clothing, increasing evaporation and removing any pockets of warmed air which remain. And finally, because he is tired and resting, the lack of muscular effort means that he is producing very little heat, with few reserves of energy to redress the balance.

In a nutshell, heat is being ripped out of his body at a rate far in excess of heat production. Unless this heat loss is checked, he will shortly become hypothermic. *See page 219.* The best way to check the heat loss – and to prevent it from occurring in the first place – is to wear the correct clothing.

## Principles of the layer system

Undoubtedly the best way to protect yourself from the elements is by using the layer system. This works on the principle that air is an excellent insulator, therefore the more layers of air you trap, the greater will be the degree of insulation. Hence the advice read in all the old mountaineering books that two thin sweaters are far better than one thick one. There is, of course, an additional advantage that it is far easier to ventilate if you wear a number of thin layers than would be the case if you were to wear just one thick one. Although in its most basic form the layer system simply involves wearing a number of garments, each of which traps one or more layers of air, the make-up of these layers bears closer scrutiny for there are three main components.

First comes the inner layer worn next to the skin. This is followed by one or more thermal layers, the number depending upon the insulation value of the garments worn (often quoted in terms of a Tog Value), and the time of year or ambient temperatures expected. All these layers are then enclosed with any one of a number of different types of outer shell. Finally, you should not forget some form of protection for the extremities – the hands, head and, of course, the feet.

## Inner layer

The innermost layer, which comes into contact with the skin, is perhaps the most misunderstood of all the layers. Its major role is that of wicking the moisture of perspiration away from the body to leave a dry layer next to the skin. In this way it plays a major role in helping to reduce the possibility of heat loss through conduction.

Of all the modern materials on the market, arguably the best for the inner layer is that made from 100% polypropylene, as will be the case with the vast majority of good quality thermal underwear. Of the more traditional materials, wool and silk are unbeatable, although many people find wool unbearable when worn against the skin.

When buying garments for your inner layer, no matter whether to clothe the upper or lower part of your body, it is worth giving the fit a little thought. Close-fitting, body-hugging garments work far better than loose fitting ones, but beware the dangers of chafing, especially around the tops of the inner thighs, under the arms, and around the pectorals. Make sure, also, that they restrict neither movement nor circulation.

Design, too, is worth considering. Depending upon the time of year when you are most likely to use the garment, it may be better to purchase a long-sleeved vest rather than a T-shirt design. Similarly, if you visit a well-stocked shop, you will probably be faced with a range of collar designs, the most common being polo-neck (with or without a short zip), crew-neck or V-neck. My personal preference for the colder months is a polo-neck with a short zip. This enables me to zip up the collar to give my neck some protection during draughty times, whilst still allowing me to open the front slightly in order to ventilate when necessary. However, what is right for me is not necessarily going to be best for you. So long as the garment does the job it is required to do (i.e. wicks moisture away from the skin) the next most important consideration has to be that of personal comfort.

## Thermal layer

After the inner layer comes the thermal layer. The purpose of this layer is to trap air so as to form an insulating barrier between you and the outside elements. This barrier can be made up from one or more garments, the number obviously depending upon the time of year and/or the severity of the conditions. However, it is no good wearing several insulating layers if the first gust of wind passes through them and replaces warm air with cold, so although you will often be wearing a windproof outer shell, it is not a bad idea to include some fairly wind-resistant garments in this layer.

Looking at the natural materials, wool is again a good choice which has the added advantage of retaining much insulation even when wet. Wet wool can actually emit a small amount of heat due to a complex chemical reaction. However, wool is heavy and bulky, and will absorb an alarming amount of water making it even heavier. It also takes a long time to dry out. Additionally, although some of the more closely woven materials have a high degree of wind resistance, your standard "woolly-pully" is not going to keep you warm on a windy day unless you wear a shell garment over the top!

Although wool has its devotees, it is probably fair to say that it has nowadays been largely replaced by modern fleece materials. These, too, retain their insulation properties when wet, but they are weight-for-weight warmer than wool, and are generally less bulky. Additionally, most fabrics absorb very little water (particularly those made from polyester and acrylic), which means they also dry remarkably quickly. Regarding wind-resistance, it is usual to find that the thicker, softer and more "snuggly" the fleece, the less it will be able to cut the wind. Thus although the thinner fleeces may not be as warm, weight-for-weight, as the thicker ones, they may be found more efficient on a breezy day in late spring or early autumn when the ambient temperature is not too cold. When out buying, the simplest way to compare the wind resistance of two fleece jackets is to blow through a layer of fabric on each.

Some manufacturers offer fleece garments with some form of inner or outer lining (such as Pertex) which will increase the wind resistance (and the price) quite significantly. Such garments fall into a grey area between that of thermal layer garments and outer shell garments. I do not mean this in any derogatory way – many of these designs are extremely useful and practical – but they should not be seen as an exclusive substitute for either of these other two layers.

Regarding thermal layers for the lower half of the body, exactly the same considerations apply although most people do not like to insulate their legs too much. This is almost certainly due to the fact that the legs do a lot of work in the mountains and the muscular effort therefore generates a fair amount of heat. Lightweight walking trousers made of polycotton or similar fabrics are extremely popular, as are the ubiquitous Trackster types. On colder days it is easy to add another layer either with thermal long-johns or a pair of tights, or you can test the theory of insulating by trapping air by wearing two pairs of Tracksters (it works!). For those really cold days, fleece trousers are superb; and if there is also a bitter wind blowing, try a pair of walking trousers lined with fleece.

As with the inner layer, the design of the garments can play an important part. All should be reasonably close fitting without there being any restriction of body movement, especially if you intend to do any scrambling or climbing. There must also be no restriction of blood circulation, and this is particularly important in cold, winter conditions where any restriction of circulation can lead to several problems including frostbite. More generally, there should be a good overlap between upper and lower garments in the area around the kidneys and the waist in order to prevent cold spots. Bearing this in mind, for severe winter use, or use when scrambling and climbing, salopettes (romper-suits for adults) are ideal, and these are available in a number of materials for use either as part of a thermal layer or part of an outer shell.

The ability to ventilate is important, and this is best done via full- or half-length front zips in at least some of the garments. Shirts can be useful here, too. It may be found useful if the design of the cuffs allows the sleeves to be pushed or rolled up slightly without cutting off the circulation, but this is very much a matter of personal preference along with such things as elasticated waists and pockets. The shape of the neck-line, too, is really a matter of personal taste, although it is worth bearing in mind that it is possible to lose a considerable amount of heat from around an open neck if a garment is loose-fitting. Finally, it goes without saying that all this clothing should feel comfortable.

## Traditional outer shells

It is of little use wearing efficient inner and thermal layers if the first draught of wind cuts through them and blows away all the warmed air, or if the first drop of rain soaks you to the skin. Therefore to finish off your protection from the elements you need an effective outer shell. When I first started visiting the mountains it was necessary to carry two different types of shell garment – a windproof anorak and a waterproof cagoule. A traditional windproof anorak is made from one or more layers of closely-woven, cotton-based material, the best (and most expensive) being Ventile (see later). Whilst many of these garments are water-resistant, few are waterproof. This is an important difference.

Anoraks and more modern windproof walking jackets should be roomy enough to go over your inner and thermal layers without restricting movement or constricting circulation. They should be cut long enough to cover the buttocks, and should have a large hood which comfortably covers the head even when you are wearing a hat. It should be able to accommodate a helmet if you intend to do any rock climbing, serious scrambling, or winter mountaineering. Some hoods are detachable, being held in place by press studs. If you choose this style of jacket, make sure that the press-studs offer a positive attachment and are positioned in such a way that there is no chance of getting draughts down the back of your neck. Other useful features include storm cuffs (elasticated inner cuffs) or some form of end-of-sleeve closure, plus at least one zipped or well-baffled pocket large enough to hold an Ordnance Survey map.

Two basic styles of garment are available. Those based on a jacket design should have full length zips, and it is well worth paying a little extra to get good-quality, large-toothed, two-way zips. These are far less prone to jamming or breaking, and the ability to unzip the jacket both from the top and the bottom can be extremely useful.

The zips should be covered with a strip of material (a baffle) in order to draught-proof them, and many jackets will have a zipped inner pocket which is accessible from behind the baffle. This is extremely useful as it allows you to access the pocket in bad weather without unzipping the jacket. Beware of jackets with unbaffled zips (very draughty), or with seams across the shoulders (a weak-point which can also be uncomfortable when carrying heavy rucksacks). Windproof garments based on the more traditional anorak design only have a half-length zip and are put on and taken off over the head – a manoeuvre which can have fairly obvious attend-ant risks if done when standing on a narrow ledge above a significant drop in windy weather! The better designs will have a well-baffled zip and a large front pouch pocket (also zipped and baffled). Storm cuffs and large hood should be as per the jacket styles, whilst many will have a drawstring at the waist and possibly a crutch-strap to stop the garment rising in strong winds. Although you should aim to wear trousers or breeches which have a fair degree of wind resistance, it is possible to buy windproof overtrousers. Whilst many people will argue that these are essential in windy winter conditions, especially in the Scottish Highlands, the better ones are fairly expensive items and it is nowadays probably more cost effective (and equally effective) to buy a pair of overtrousers made from a breathable waterproof fabric *(see later)*.

Because standard cotton-based windproof fabrics are rarely 100% waterproof, it is necessary for you to have a set of waterproof clothing as well. For serious mountain use this should include both jacket and overtrousers. There are two problems here. Firstly, it appears that different manufacturers have differing ideas about what constitutes a "100% waterproof" fabric! Secondly, any fabric that really is 100% waterproof will not allow body moisture to escape and you will therefore get wet simply by wearing it – even on a dry day! Most newcomers to mountain activities are amazed at the amount of condensation which can occur in this way; if you are not sure yourself try running around your garden wearing a plastic bin-liner!

The traditional waterproof garment was the cagoule – basically a long nylon sack with arms and a hood. Unlike anoraks which are still to be seen gracing the backs of centrebound schoolchildren and yomping soldiers, the cagoule has largely been replaced by a more conventional waterproof jacket.

Modern waterproof jackets are usually made from nylon material which has been coated with a waterproofing agent, the most common being either neoprene or (better) polyurethane (pu). These coatings will not last indefinitely and, generally speaking, the lighter the material they proof, the quicker they will wear away. The lightest practical fabric is 2oz nylon, but I would advise you to choose something substantially heavier than this (at least 7oz) if you intend to walk in the mountains with any regularity. The jacket should be long enough to reach the base of the buttocks and, as with windproof jackets, the front opening should be closed with a well-baffled, large-toothed, two-way zip. Similarly, there should be no seams across the shoulders as these represent weak spots which will soon leak, no matter how well proofed they are initially.

All seams should be sealed in some way, the best method being hot-taping. The hood, which should be large enough to accommodate a woolly hat or, if necessary, a climbing helmet, should have a drawstring so that it can be pulled tight around the face, and it helps to have a wire reinforcement at the top (to enhance vision) and a front zip which extends well up towards the mouth. If, like me, you are bearded, make sure there is a beard-guard or some form of internal baffle. From painful experience I can assure you that getting large clumps of beard caught in the teeth of a zip is not an experience you would wish to go through twice!

In addition to a waterproof jacket, you will also need a pair of waterproof overtrousers. These should not be regarded as an optional extra but as an essential item of mountain clothing. A good pair of overtrousers will be fairly roomy, and will be cut in such a way that they cause no restriction of movement – especially when bending the legs at the knees. This is particularly important if you intend to do any scrambling, rock climbing or winter mountaineering. You should also be able to put on and take off the trousers without having to remove your boots, and this is usually accomplished either by having a baffled zip or (better) a large zipped gusset, extending from the bottom of the leg to just below the knees.

As mentioned earlier, any material which is 100% waterproof will prevent body moisture escaping. If, for example, you wear your waterproof shell on a mild, misty day, you will end up getting wetter from condensation than you would from the mist. But it is still better to wear your waterproofs than not because they provide a barrier to evaporation and thus drastically reduce the potential heat loss. Also, because waterproof fabrics are almost invariably windproof, your waterproof garments can also serve as windproof garments, even though this may not be the most comfortable of experiences.

## Modern outer shells

There can be little doubt that the advent of breathable waterproof fabrics has revolutionised outdoor clothing, and nowhere is this more apparent than in outer shell garments. Gone are the days when it was necessary to carry separate windproof and waterproof shells. Nowadays a single garment can comfortably perform both functions. However, breathable fabrics are not a wholly modern idea. Ventile – a closely woven cotton-based fabric – has been around for decades and possesses many of the features of modern breathable fabrics (including high cost). On the plus side, Ventile is extremely durable; on the minus side it is fairly heavy. The best garments are made from a double layer of the material.

Modern breathable fabrics fall into two categories: membrane (or laminated) materials and coated materials. Of the two, the membrane materials are arguably the more effective, although this is not to say that the coated materials are no good. Probably the best known membrane material is Goretex, whilst Cyclone is one of the better known coated materials. Both types of fabric can work in one of two ways. Microporous fabrics contain a material which has microscopic holes, small enough to prevent water droplets from penetrating but large enough to allow water vapour to pass. Hydrophilic fabrics contain a solid waterproof material made up from chains of water-loving molecules which allow the passage of water vapour.

Whichever type of material you choose, it will not last for ever. Coatings will eventually wear away and membranes deteriorate. Three-layer laminates (in which the membrane is sandwiched between material) are generally more durable than two layer laminates (in which the membrane is bonded to an outer material, the inner lining hanging free).

Breathable fabrics all work on a similar principle. Preventing the passage of water droplets means they are waterproof; allowing the passage of water vapour means they reduce the amount of condensation of body moisture. I use the term reduce because I have yet to come across any breathable fabric which works with 100% efficiency under mountain conditions. Firstly, any dirt will cause the performance to deteriorate (effectively, the dirt will clog the pores), so you should keep garments clean. With most fabrics, particularly the laminates, regular washing will enhance the performance, but you should follow the manufacturers washing instructions to the letter. Secondly, these fabrics will only work if the conditions inside them are warmer and more moist than the conditions outside. Taking an extreme example, if you were to wear a breathable jacket in a hot, steamy jungle, water vapour could pass from the outside to the inside!

Thirdly, if you are walking into a headwind during a rainstorm and the front of your jacket is saturated with water, it will be impossible for the water vapour to pass through. Occasionally, therefore, it is advisable to give the outer fabric a spray with a proprietary water repellent so that any water forms into droplets which are then shed before they saturate the fabric. As with washing, it is important that you follow the manufacturer's reproofing instructions because some proofing agents will have an adverse effect on laminates and original coatings.

Finally, mention should be made of some of the microfibre jackets now available. Commonly made from materials such as Pertex, these are incredibly light, will roll up into a remarkably small space, and are virtually 100% windproof. Whilst they are not waterproof, they are certainly water resistant and breathable, and can be highly effective in windy or moist, misty conditions. They are particularly suitable for use in late spring and early autumn when the ambient temperature is not too low but the wind has a definite bite to it. It goes without saying that all of these modern fabric garments should be well designed, comfortable and functional, possessing the same features as the more traditional garments.

## Protection for the extremities

There is little point in covering your torso in warm, windproof, waterproof clothing if you neglect your hands, feet, and head. Protection for the head is particularly important as you can lose up to 50% of the body's heat production from here.

The traditional protection for the head is some form of woolly hat – either a simple bobble hat or a ski hat. Whatever style you favour, your hat should be large enough to cover the ears and the base of the neck. Many hill walkers like "Inca" style hats with ear flaps. For particularly harsh weather, a balaclava is extremely useful. Brushed wool is ideal, so too are polypropylene (thermal underwear material), silk, and fleece. The more wind-resistant the balaclava, the better, even though they will often be worn inside the hood of your jacket. Paramilitary masks with separate holes for each eye and the mouth are not the most suitable of hats for the mountains as they restrict the vision and will probably get you strange, often unfriendly looks from people you meet along the way!

Also extremely useful are headovers. These are basically tubes of thermal material which can be used in a number of ways, the three most popular being round the neck as a scarf, twisted in the middle and doubled over the head as a hat, and over the head but under the jaws as a balaclava.

Protection for the hands is best obtained via mittens. These are generally far superior to gloves although they can be more cumbersome. Brushed wool mittens are excellent, as are those made from fibre-pile or fleece lined nylon. Whilst these are not waterproof they are windproof, and will retain much of their insulation value even when saturated. Waterproof thermal mittens are available (at a price), but it is probably more cost effective (and certainly more adaptable) to get a pair of thin thermal gloves *(see below)* or woollen mittens and a pair of overmitts which are both waterproof and windproof. Such a combination is essential in winter, particularly if you intend to do any serious winter mountaineering in the Scottish Highlands.

If you prefer to wear gloves, avoid those made from leather as these have very little insulation value, especially if they get wet. Wool or fleece gloves are good, as are thin gloves made from thermal-underwear material, these latter having the advantage that they can be used as liners for mittens. They are also quite useful if you need to use your hand for dextrous work (tying knots, photography, etc.). Also available for dextrous work are fingerless gloves and "shooters-mitts" or "flip-mitts" – mittens which can be opened across the knuckles to give access to the fingers.

Whatever you choose to wear, it is of vital importance that there is no restriction of circulation. Restriction of movement is one thing (your mittens, for example, may be cumbersome), but restriction of the blood flow is another matter altogether. Apart from the fact that a lack of blood flowing to the fingers will make them feel colder that much quicker, you also run the very real risk of frostbite or frostnip during winter conditions. If you intend to do any technical ice climbing, a pair of overmitts large enough to accommodate a piece of closed-cell foam across the top of the hand will help to reduce the risk of bruised knuckles!

Last but by no means least, the feet. Whatever the weather, these are best protected by wearing at least one pair of woollen socks or stockings. 100% wool socks are great, but tend to wear out fairly quickly; a 70% wool: 30% nylon mix is far more durable while still performing well. Foot care is obviously very important. What would be a minor blister around the garden can become a serious problem when you are several rough miles from civilisation and your only mode of transport is your feet.

Socks have to fulfil a number of functions. They need to provide insulation from the elements and to offer a degree of protection from the hammering you give your feet as you walk. They should also reduce the friction between your foot and your boot and absorb any perspiration. The best socks are constructed either entirely of loopstitch, or have at least a loopstitch foot. This not only insulates the foot but also affords some cushioning. People with sensitive feet may not be able to cope with heavy wool next to the skin, in which case a liner of light thermal socks or everyday socks can be worn. It has to be said that an awful lot of rubbish has been written about how many pairs of socks you should wear. The standard seems to be two, but I know of people who wear three pairs and others who wear only one pair. The bottom line here is comfort. Once again, there should be no restriction of movement or circulation – you should be able to wiggle your toes with ease.

You should keep your socks clean, washing them regularly and using a good fabric conditioner. If you wear a hole in them, throw them away or use them for gardening! It is false economy to try and darn the socks you use on the mountains for, however well they are repaired, darned socks are far more likely to cause blisters than undarned socks.

In addition to socks, shock-absorbing insoles made from closed-cell foam, or sorbothane, are very effective if you are into long distance walking or if your boots are not a snug fit. Those shaped like a footbed can give extra support to the arches and many people find them particularly good.

In wet, cold, or windy conditions, gaiters can be a boon; in winter conditions they can be essential. Apart from the fact that they will afford a certain amount of protection from the wind and rain, they are virtually essential when wearing overtrousers as they prevent the water flowing down the trouser leg and straight into the boot. Make sure you wear your gaiters underneath your over-trousers otherwise they will have the opposite effect! You can also buy waterproof socks made from a breathable material which will help keep your feet dry no matter what the weather.

Gaiters made from canvas are excellent, being durable and easily reproofed. Those made of nylon are lighter, but they tend to make your legs feel sticky, they lose their coating fairly quickly, and tend to make a surprising amount of noise! Gaiters made from breathable materials are very expensive and because they get so much punishment, they tend to loose their breathable/waterproof qualities within a remarkably short space of time. Yeti gaiters (which cover the whole boot) are excellent, although it is fair to say that their performance varies depending upon the type of boot. Certain types of boot have been designed to take certain types of Yeti gaiter, and these usually work together very well.

## Cold-weather clothing

All things being equal, if you use the layer system you should be able to cope with most conditions you will meet in the British mountains. However, there may be times, particularly north of the Scottish border in the winter months, when a little extra protection will be useful. At one time duvet jackets were the trademark of the serious mountain-eer. Nowadays they are commonplace in city streets, but many of the models available from the High

Street stores are more fashionable than functional. Even those designed specifically for mountain use come in various styles with different inner and outer fabrics and a range of fillings.

For example, few of the cheaper duvet jackets are waterproof, and for this reason it may not be the best idea to buy a duvet jacket filled with down – for although this is a superb insulator, it loses its insulation properties when wet. Admittedly, it is possible to buy down duvet jackets with a water-proof (or breathable) outer fabric, but these cost a king's ransom and will probably be beyond the means of all but the most committed mountaineers. It is also possible to proof a down duvet jacket using a total-immersion waterproofing compound.

For most people, duvet jackets with a totally synthetic filling (usually of spun polyester fibres) are generally more functional, although unless you spend a lot of money they will also be heavier and more bulky. Having said this, bulk is quite important in a duvet jacket. Although it is possible to buy jackets lined with very effective thin insulation such as Thinsulate, they somehow do not feel so warm. Psychology plays a large part when it comes to feeling warm! Whilst duvet jackets are obviously useful, especially when resting, particularly in an emergency or a survival situation, they are often too hot to wear whilst moving. An alternative is to buy a body warmer – a duvet jacket without arms.

As was mentioned earlier, it is possible to buy lined fleece jackets, the lining usually being of polycotton or (better), of a windproof, water-shedding material such as Pertex. Many of these are reversible. If you wear them with the lining on the outside they will be warmer than if you wear them with the lining on the inside, simply because the lining acts as a barrier to the breeze and prevents the escape of warm air. Many manufacturers offer a range of interactive jackets which zip one inside the other. Thus you can buy a waterproof jacket and a fleece jacket and either wear them singly or zip them together to form a single garment.

Finally, salopettes (adult romper-suits) are ideal in really cold conditions or when you think you may be hanging around. These are available in a range of styles (long leg, breeches leg, bib top, sleeveless, etc.) and a variety of materials, including fibre-pile, fleece, and breathable waterproof fabric. It is even possible to buy quilted salopettes filled with down.

## Hot-weather clothing

British weather being what it is, you are more likely to meet cold, wet and windy weather than a heat wave. However, there may be the occasional day when the sun beats down and all you want to do is keep cool. In these conditions there is no reason at all why you should not wear shorts and a T-shirt – so long as you carry clothing to cover your arms and legs with you in your rucksack.

Although some people like to wear running vests, you should beware the possibility of sore shoulders caused by rubbing rucksack straps. Additionally, no matter how well you can soak up the sun in the valleys, when walking in the mountains in hot, sunny weather you should carry a good quality sun-screen – and use it regularly.

Another essential item of clothing in hot, sunny weather is some form of sunhat. This should preferably be light both in colour and weight, with a wide brim to shade the eyes and give protection to the back of the neck. In the same way as hypothermia is a risk in cold, wet weather, heat-stroke is a very real risk in hot weather.

## Footwear

It would be possible to devote a whole book to footwear suitable for the mountains. All I can hope to do here is give you a run-down of the basic types and the pros and cons of each. As with many other aspects of mountaincraft, what is important is that you understand the basics. You can then visit your local, friendly gear retailer to get the details and see the latest developments. A further problem is that there is no such thing as the ideal footwear for all occasions, so you either have to compromise and buy a general purpose boot or shell out and buy two or more pairs. For example, a pair of fully stiffened plastic boots, although ideal for winter mountaineering, is less than perfect for summer hillwalking.

First and foremost, you should be thinking in terms of boots – NOT shoes. Sturdy walking shoes may be okay for valley walks, but they do not give sufficient ankle support for walking across rough terrain. Recently some experienced mountaineers have been extolling the virtues of specialist trekking sandals. Whilst these may be all right for the experts in particular situations, (or for use when knocking about camp), in my opinion most of us lesser mortals do not have sufficient ankle strength to make sandals a particularly wise choice for wear in the mountains.

Your footwear probably represents the most significant mountain activities purchase you will ever make. So far as I am concerned, as long as the basic functions outlined below are fulfilled, the most important consideration is that of comfort; it is pointless buying a pair of expensive boots if they start to hurt your feet after a couple of miles. The fit is absolutely vital, so take your time when buying. You should also either take along the socks you normally wear when on the hill, buy some new socks to go with the new boots, or get the shop to loan you a pair of socks similar to your own.

If the shop you are in is worth visiting, you should not feel hurried. Indeed, buying a pair of boots will probably take an hour or more during which time you will have tried on a few different types and sizes and (if the shop is particularly good) will probably have been offered a mug of coffee! Furthermore, the best shops will allow you to exchange your boots within a week or so as long as you have only worn them around the house. Bearing all this in mind, I strongly recommend against buying boots by mail order.

In addition to general comfort there are a few things to note when choosing a size. If your heel moves up and down as you walk then the boot is slightly too large. This may lead to blisters on the back of the heel – a common complaint. If your toes feel at all cramped then the boot is too narrow a fit, and not only do you run the risk of blisters across the tops and sides of your toes, but walking could become excruciatingly painful after a few miles of rough terrain. If you can feel the end of the boot with your toes when you stamp your foot forward, then the boot is too small, and not only will descents prove painful, but you also run the very real risk of losing your toenails.

Regarding the method of construction and the style of boot, there are a number of aspects worth noting, one of the more important being the stiffness of the sole. Although personal preference will play a part, a good rule of thumb is that the rougher the terrain across which you intend to travel, the stiffer and more substantial should be the sole. Additionally, if you intend to do any winter mountaineering using crampons, you will need a boot robust enough to cope with step kicking with a fully stiffened sole.

There is little doubt that fabric boots of virtually any description are unsuitable for serious mountain use, the main reason being that they give insufficient ankle support. Additionally, all but a few are too flexible, and most are far from waterproof. Even if you spend a lot of money on boots made from a breathable waterproof fabric, in my experience the membrane cannot stand up to constant hammering and breaks down remarkably quickly. Having said all this, I know of highly experienced mountaineers who extol the virtues of this type of boot.

A good, general purpose boot suitable for mountain walking, scrambling and simple rock climbing will be a medium-weight leather boot which, although difficult to bend by hand, flexes slightly across the ball of the foot. Such a boot is often described as having a three-quarters shank. In addition to stiffness along the foot, there should also be a high degree of stiffness across the foot, and the sole should be thick enough to cushion the feet from sharp stones and pebbles. If you hold the boot at the heel and the toe, it should resist any twisting motion.

The sole should be made of a rubber compound in preference to the cheaper PVC, and the tread pattern should be of the traditional "vibram" type or the more modern "monobloc". The welt (the projection of the sole around the boot) should be narrow. Beware those soles with cut-away heels – there is a growing evidence to suggest that the grip given by these soles is inferior to that of more traditional designs, especially in descent. Although a good pair of boots will grip well in most circumstances assuming you are placing your feet correctly (*see page 76*), both traditional and modern soles do have their limitations. In particular they have a notoriously bad grip on greasy rock, hard packed snow and ice, and (more surprisingly, perhaps) on grass which is either very wet or very dry.

The method by which the sole is attached to the boot is fairly important. Most soles are either sewn, glued, screwed or welded to the upper (usually via a mid-sole), and many manufacturers use a combination of two or more of these methods. If you choose a boot with welded soles you will find it difficult if not impossible to have it resoled. Additionally, boots with welded soles often lack tortional rigidity. The leather from which the uppers are made should be of good quality, and there should be as few seams as possible – the best (and most expensive) boots will be made from a single piece of leather, the only seams being at the heel and the tongue. The more seams there are, the weaker and potentially less waterproof the boot. A sewn-in or bellows tongue is essentially to prevent the ingress of water, and the most convenient form of lacing uses two forms of attachment: D-rings (which hold the laces in place at the forward part of the boot) and speed-hooks (which enable you to get in and out of the boot without too much difficulty).

If you intend to do any winter mountaineering your boot will need to be particularly robust, with a higher degree of longitudinal rigidity (full shank). Traditional winter mountaineering boots are very heavy – nowadays the lighter, warmer plastic boots have become the norm. Consisting essentially of two boots in one – a flat-soled, flexible inner boot made of leather, and a rigid plastic outer boot, usually with a Vibram-type sole – these boots bear all the hallmarks and features of a top quality leather boot. They have many advantages, not the least of which are ease of maintenance and the fact that the boot is about as waterproof as it can possibly be.

## Boot care

Once you have chosen your footwear, you will obviously want it to last as long as possible. After each sojourn into the hills, remove any mud which may have clogged the treads by holding the boots at the ankle and banging the soles together. Check the condition of the laces, replacing them as necessary, and tease out any small stones from the treads using a blunt instrument (the handle of a teaspoon is ideal). Remove dirt from the uppers with a nail brush and damp cloth. With plastic boots, there is very little else to do, but leather boots will need to be reproofed occasionally. First, allow the boots to dry out slowly. Stuff them with newspaper and leave them in an airy place. On no account try to accelerate the drying process by leaving wet boots in drying rooms, on top of radiators or near fires, for this will cause the leather to buckle and harden. In extreme cases it may even become brittle and crack.

When dry, leather boots should be given a coating of good quality wax polish or a proprietary reproofing compound such as Nikwax, with particular attention being paid to the seams. Water-based proofings are particularly good as they seek out those places in most need of reproofing, giving them proportionally more protection. Avoid using liquid conditioners over prolonged periods as these will soften the leather causing excessive wear. Such liquid proofings can also become concentrated beneath the stitching with the inevitable result that the leather will soften sufficiently for the stitches to cut through.

Finally, because leather contains natural oils which are lost through time, especially if it becomes saturated with water, your boots will benefit from an occasional dose of a specialist leather conditioner.

# 2  Hill walking equipment

As with clothing and footwear, there are few hard and fast rules about what you should take with you when you go into the hills. Your choice of equipment will depend upon many factors including what you intend to attempt, prevailing weather, time of year, location, etc. Whilst there are a few essential items, striking the right balance between comfort and safety can be quite difficult, and it is fair to say that there are as many people who take too much with them as there are people who take too little.

In this section we are going to look at those items which most people consider to be the bare essentials for summer mountain walking, and describe a range of other items, some of which are essential in winter conditions, and others which may simply make life more comfortable.

It is worth bearing in mind that everything you take you have to carry. The more you carry, the slower you will be and the more energy you will use up. Because conservation of energy is an important consideration whenever you visit the mountains, there inevitably comes a time when carrying extra "safety" equipment becomes counter-productive.

A good way to put this all into perspective is to ask whether you could survive an unexpected night on the mountains. Not to put too fine a point on it, the chances of an ill-equipped, inexperienced party surviving a forced benightment in the Scottish hills in winter are negligible.

## Essential items

There are few really essential items of equipment. In addition to the clothing and footwear you wear, you should always carry a spare sweater (or similar), a full set of waterproofs, a pair of gloves or mittens, and a hat *(see section 1)*. These should be carried in a good-quality rucksack – not as is all too often seen, in a plastic carrier bag! Unless you are only going for a half day walk of a couple of miles or less, you should also take something to eat and something to drink. No matter what your plans, you should have the relevant map(s) and an orient-eering or protractor compass *(see page 144)*, a watch, and a whistle.

Additionally, lodged permanently in your rucksack and taken on every trip there should be a survival bag, some form of emergency food, and, at the very least, a basic first aid kit. Please note that this is the basic kit for mountain walking in summer conditions. From autumn to spring you should add a headtorch and batteries to your list. In winter you will need additional spare clothing including a pair of gaiters, and if there is any sign of snow an ice axe should be regarded as an absolute necessity *(see below and on page 104)*. Additionally, during the winter months, at least one person in the party should carry a sleeping bag.

No matter what the time of year, if you intend to

do any scrambling you should take a rope and possibly a helmet *(as described on page 79)*.

Of course, the bottom line is that none of this equipment possesses any magical properties of its own, so it is pointless carrying any of it unless you know how to use it.

## Daysacks

There is nothing to beat the convenience and practicality of having a small rucksack in which to carry your essential gear. Whilst waist pouches and bum bags may be perfectly adequate for low-level valley walks, they are not really suitable for more serious mountain walking. Many do not have sufficient capacity, and those that do tend to be cumbersome and unwieldy. However, a daysack which is too large is almost as much a problem as one which is too small because most people find there is an almost irresistible temptation to fill it to capacity.

Rucksack capacity is quoted in litres, daysacks typically ranging from about 20 to 50 litres. The further you intend to walk, the rougher the terrain or the more extreme the weather, the larger the capacity of daysack you will need. For summer mountain walking you will need a daysack of between 25 and 35 litres. If you intend to do any scrambling or rock work, a capacity of between 30 and 40 litres would be useful. If you intend to visit the mountains under winter conditions you should be thinking in terms of 40 to 50 litres. Many models are available with compression straps. These allow you to alter the capacity of the daysack according to your needs, this facility making the daysack extremely versatile.

Daysacks should be functional, and the simpler the design, the better. The main body of the daysack is best formed from a rectangular box-shaped bag of waterproof material, nylon-based fabrics being ideal. Some manufacturers have developed their own specialist rucksack fabrics and offer a lifetime guarantee. There should be few seams (seams represent weak-points in terms of both strength and water resistance), and those that there are should be strongly sewn. It is worth checking the quality of the stitching as this varies widely from manufacturer to manufacturer.

The top of the daysack should be fitted with an efficient drawcord, the whole of this area then being covered by a large flap. This should have elasticated sides and should be shaped to fit snugly over the top of the daysack in order to keep out the majority of any precipitation. Although this may look effective, and despite the claims of many manufacturers, I have yet to come across any rucksack which is 100% waterproof in a mountain storm.

Even if the material is waterproof, there are so many stress points (not to mention a large hole at the top!) that water is bound to seep in somewhere. It is therefore prudent to pack any items you wish to keep dry (such as spare clothing) in a plastic bag before putting them into your sack.

Alternatively, if you suspect the material may not be 100% waterproof you can use a rucksack liner –

little more than a heavy-duty bin-liner. An empty (washed) fertiliser sack begged from a farmer does just as well, and doesn't cost!

The design of the shoulder straps and the method used to connect them to the main body of the daysack is obviously of critical importance. The straps themselves should be well-padded and at least 5cms wide. They will obviously need to be adjustable, and this is best done via non-slip friction buckles which are placed in such a position that they can be adjusted while on the move.

You should aim to adjust the straps so that the load is carried as high as possible on the back, the weight bearing directly downwards. A light waist-strap is useful when scrambling or crossing rough terrain, and some people find a chest-strap useful on the larger day-sacks.

The method of attachment should be sturdy and durable, the shoulder straps being firmly attached to the main body of the daysack, preferably with some reinforcement. It is useful to have a haul-strap or webbing loop which can be used as a handle . If the straps are set too close together there is the risk that they may cut into the back of your neck, and for this reason it is better to avoid those daysacks which are pear-shaped or triangular. In any case, such designs are to be avoided as they do not allow you to carry the load high on your back *(see section 4)*.

A low load results in a bad posture in which you are bent forward using your back and shoulder muscles. This can be extremely fatiguing. A high load results in an upright posture in which the weight bears directly downwards onto the pelvic girdle and onto the legs. Long straps and large external pockets have an infuriating habit of becoming snagged at the most inconvenient times, and you would do well to avoid any daysack which is covered in pockets or has vast lengths of webbing all over it.

However, one or two pockets can be extremely convenient for carrying any items which you might use regularly or need to hand, and some of the better daysacks have a shallow pouch pocket across the front, or two compact sides pockets. If you intend to go scrambling or rock climbing it would be better to avoid daysacks with side pockets as they are more unwieldy than those without.

Many manufacturers incorporate a pouch pocket in the top flap, and this can be extremely useful. For obvious reasons, all pockets should be zipped and baffled. To save the apprehensive key-searching at the end of a long day, a few daysacks are available with small zipped key-pockets in which you can keep car keys, money, etc.

One problem with wearing a daysack for any length of time, especially on a warm day, is that condensation builds up across your back. This is particularly marked if the daysack is made from nylon fabric. Although most manufacturers have gone to some lengths in an attempt to reduce this problem in their backpacking rucksacks, few have done so with daysacks, although some use canvas or a similar material for the back panel. It has to be said that this is a less than perfect solution.

# Food and drink

Due to the combination of fresh air and sometimes strenuous exercise, most people get ravenously hungry when visiting the mountains. Even if you do not feel hungry it is vital to maintain your energy reserves, so it is important to take the right food with you. This is even more critical if you are camping *(see section 5)*. You should aim to get a balanced diet which provides you with a minimum of 4000 kilocalories of energy per day.

By far the most important meal of the day is breakfast. A common misconception is that sugars are the best source of energy. Although sugars are rich in quickly available energy, in fact it is fats which are the richest source of energy, so a good old-fashioned fry-up is highly recommended. However, it takes time for the body to get to the energy locked in fats, so it is best to have a leisurely breakfast a good hour before taking to the hills.

Packed lunches for consumption on the hill should contain a high proportion of carbohydrates (i.e. sugars and starches). Although weight-for-weight these do not contain as much energy as fats, the energy they do contain is available to the body almost immediately. Sugars are the more effective of the two, so trail snacks (to be eaten whilst actively walking) should have a high sugar content. Choose something that you enjoy eating, not too heavy in weight and easily digestible.

Try to consume little and often. Stopping for an hour in the middle and consuming all your food may appear to be refreshing, but it is not the best way of keeping up your energy. Not only will your food lie heavy on your stomach, but long stops break your body's natural rhythm making you feel lethargic and stiff afterwards.

For most people, the evening meal will be the major meal of the day. If you are camping or visiting the mountains again the following day, this should be a substantial meal with at least one hot course which boosts energy reserves.

Many people seriously underestimate the amount of liquid they should drink whilst active in the hills. Indeed, dehydration is a far more common complaint than most people realise. Although it is possible to go into water-debt for short periods without too many ill effects, it is not good practice. Liquid is required in order to metabolise energy, so you should aim to maintain a good water balance. During mountain walking in temperate conditions you should aim to consume about 4 litres of liquid per day. Considerably more than this may be needed if you are undertaking particularly strenuous walks or if the weather is hot. As with eating, little and often is the best policy. Consuming large quantities of liquid whilst on the move will make you feel heavy and could lead to stomach cramp. Consuming large quantities of liquid in a local inn in order to "rehydrate" is an essential part of many people's day, but bear in mind that alcohol has diuretic properties and is therefore not the most efficient way of maintaining the correct balance!

In hot weather, some form of electrolyte replacement drink is beneficial; in really cold weather a flask of hot drink can be a great morale booster and may even be a life-saver in an emergency. Contrary to popular belief, most high mountain streams and springs are perfectly safe to drink from.

You will obviously need something in which to carry all this liquid, and there is little to beat a purpose made water flask. If choosing one made from high-density plastic, check that it has a well-threaded screw top with good seals. If choosing one made from aluminium, check that it is lacquered internally, especially if you intend to use it for fruit juices or cordials. Vacuum flasks are good not only for keeping hot drinks hot, but also for keeping cold drinks cold. Those with glass inners are fairly light in weight and relatively cheap, but they vary considerably in efficiency and are obviously fragile. Far more efficient, but also far heavier and far more expensive, are unbreakable stainless-steel flasks. Whatever type you choose, it will work better if you prime it with boiling or iced water (as appropriate) for at least 5 minutes before filling. If you are camping you will have with you a stove, in which case a vacuum flask is not strictly necessary. Nevertheless, it is still a convenient item of equipment which many will find indispensable.

## Survival bags

A survival bag is an essential item of equipment which should reside permanently in your rucksack along with some survival rations (see below). This is basically a heavy-duty polythene sack about 1 metre wide and 2.5 metres long. Double versions

(1.2 metres x 2.4 metres approx.) are also available. If travelling in a group, everyone should have one. In emergency situations, particularly with hypothermic casualties, they provide shelter from the wind and drastically reduce heat loss through evaporation *(see page 17)*. It is worth noting that whilst bivouac sacks (bivi-bags) made from breathable waterproof materials can be extremely useful, they should not be carried as an alternative to a polythene survival bag simply because they allow water vapour to pass and will not, therefore, reduce heat loss through evaporation to anywhere near the same degree.

Hypothermic casualties have little body heat. Thus the popular silver space blankets which reduce heat loss by reflecting body heat and do not enclose the casualty (thus allowing draughts as well) are about as useful as a chocolate fireguard.

## Survival rations

Speaking of chocolate brings us nicely to survival rations. These should take the form of high energy foodstuffs containing a high proportion of sugars. Chocolate bars (Mars bars seem almost universally popular), mintcake, dextrose tablets, dried fruit, glucose sweets and similar items are ideal. Although ready-made survival packs are available, it is far cheaper to make up your own, and it is a good idea to choose things you like.

Such items tend to have an almost irresistible attraction during a long day on the hill. The temptation to raid them can lead to occasional pilfering with the result that you find them gone when you really need them. The best way around this problem is to place them in a large plastic sandwich bag and seal them up with a whole roll of sticky tape.

## First aid kits

At least one member of any group visiting the hills should have a good first aid kit and should have had some basic first aid training. However, it is better if every member of the party carries their own first aid kit, however basic this may be. It is also useful if at least one person carries a waxed luggage label and a chinagraph pencil. This can easily be carried in the first aid kit and, in the event of an emergency requiring evacuation by a mountain rescue team, can be used to note down the details which will be required *(see page 237)*.

## Watches

At least one person in any party visiting the mountains should have a reliable watch. Not only is this an essential item for accurate poor-visibility navigation, but because it is easy to lose all track of time in the mountains it can also be useful as an aid to preventing accidental benightment.

## Maps and compasses

No matter what the weather nor how well you think you know an area, you should always carry a suitable compass and the relevant maps when you visit the mountains. Full details are given in section

6. The time when efficient use of map and compass can become critical is during bad conditions, but it is of little use taking a map if it ends up as a soggy mass or is torn to shreds by the wind. Some form of map protection is therefore vital. Laminated maps are available, and some of the more modern of these are excellent being neither as bulky nor as unwieldy as their predecessors. Also available are "sticky" flexible plastic map cases sealed by rolling the plastic and then securing with a Velcro strip. Designed originally for canoe touring, these are weatherproof and durable, and far better than some of the cheaper versions which use a less flexible plastic which quickly becomes brittle and cracks. At the very minimum you should carry your map in a large plastic bag, preferably with some form of weathertight seal.

Wearing your map case on a lanyard around your neck is useful in that it keeps the map to hand, but you will soon become disillusioned with it in windy weather as it spins round and tries to strangle you. I find it far more convenient to keep mine underneath the shoulder strap of my rucksack.

## Whistles

A whistle should be regarded as an essential item of emergency equipment for mountain and moorland walking. The sound of a whistle will carry a long way so it can be used for gaining the attention of others if you find yourself in difficulties. The International Mountain Distress Signal is six goods blasts on a whistle followed by a minute's silence, repeated ad nauseam. The answering call is three good blasts followed by a minute"s silence, also repeated. Both signals can also be made using other media such as flashing a torch, shouting help, waving a bright object (such as a survival bag), etc. Over the past few years there has been occasional controversy in the letters pages of the specialist press regarding what is the correct distress signal. Suffice it to say that any whistling in the mountains is likely to provoke some form of investigation, so only use your whistle in emergency.

## Flares

The standard mountain distress flare is the 2 star red. These are not freely available, are quite bulky and very expensive. Because of the escape velocity of the flare when fired, you will also need a firearms certificate. If you are a casual walker and you think you ought to buy one – forget it!

More freely available are mini-flares. These usually come in mixed packs containing mainly red flares (emergency) with two or three white flares (signalling) and a pen-type launcher. The problem is that their elevation (the height they attain when fired) is not very great, and this is particularly true in windy conditions when they have all the qualities of a cheap squib. In any case, even if the weather and visibility is fine when you fire your flare, someone has to be looking in the right direction at the right time to see it, and has to have the wherewithal to note down the direction. Needless to say, I am not a great fan, and believe they have minimal use as a method of attracting attention. Having said this, they may be useful after the alarm has been raised in guiding rescuers to a precise location.

## Pedometers

Many walkers swear by pedometers, liking to know how far they have walked during the day. It is, of course, far cheaper to measure this on the map. Additionally, pedometers are nowhere near accurate enough to be used with any great advantage in navigation, especially when micro-navigating in poor visibility. If you find one useful, wear it, but it is certainly not an essential item of equipment.

## Torches

If you are visiting the mountains in autumn, winter or spring you should carry a reliable torch with good quality alkaline batteries. Winter mountain days, in particular, are very short, and a small error in navigation or unexpected delay can lead to a dangerous descent in gathering twilight or, worse, to benightment.

The most practical torches for mountain use are headtorches which not only allow you to have both hands free, but also have the advantage that the light goes where you look. Best known are those made by Petzl, which have the battery case at the back of the headband (counterbalancing the weight of the lamp) and storage space for at least one spare bulb in the lamp housing. Three different types of bulb are available: standard, long-life (less light but more battery life), and halogen (more light but less battery life). Halogen bulbs are useful if you decide to walk out; long-life bulbs are useful if you decide to sit it out. If there is a storage facility for more than one spare bulb you can carry one of each.

There is no point in carrying a torch without batteries. When in transit, keep torch and batteries separate or insert the batteries in such a way that the torch cannot be switched on accidentally. Alkaline batteries give longer life than standard batteries but are considerably heavier. It is worth noting that alkaline batteries will leak or may even explode if they are short-circuited. It is also worth bearing in mind that batteries have a shelf life. If in doubt, take a spare.

## Altimeters

Altimeters can be extremely useful although, again, they are not essential. Altimeters work by sensing changes in barometric pressure and this has a number of consequences. Firstly, you must set your altimeter at the beginning of each walk (usually by setting start height not start pressure!). Secondly, during frontal conditions when the barometric pressure may be changing fairly rapidly, they can become inaccurate, so the weather must be taken into consideration. Finally, comparing a known height with the height indicated at that point by your altimeter can give you an idea of changes in barometric pressure, and this can be of help when judging likely changes in the prevailing weather *(see also section 7)*.

## Walking sticks

Walking sticks are rightly becoming increasingly popular. They can be of great help when crossing rough terrain such as boulder fields, and during ascent and descent. They take strain off the knees and spine, and generally aid balance.

Although an old fashioned wooden stick will do the job, far better are telescopic sticks based on ski-mountaineering poles. These can be adjusted to the most comfortable and supportive length no matter whether in ascent, descent, or traverse, and can be folded down and carried along the side of your daysack (especially easy if it has compression straps) when not in use.

## Ice axes

No matter what conditions are like in the valley, an ice axe is an essential item of safety equipment if there is any sign of snow on the hill. It is not a tool purely for climbers, nor is it a luxury item. More-over, if you meet lying snow unexpectedly when you are on the hill and have no ice axe, you may have to detour around it, even if this means retracing your steps.

The biggest cause of winter accidents is simple slips on easy ground. Let me illustrate this with a typical scenario. It is a cold, crisp winter day with perfect weather. A walker is traversing a gentle (10°) slope on which there is fairly hard-packed snow. There are no steep slopes or crags anywhere around. Because the slight breeze has a bite to it, the walker is wearing his jacket and overtrousers. Paying more attention to the view than to his foot placement, he stumbles over a slightly protruding boulder, falls over and starts to slide.

The snow is too hard-packed for him to gain any purchase with his hands or feet, his clothing offers little friction, so he begins to pick up speed. By the time he has travelled 50 metres or so he is going at a considerable rate of knots (60kph+!). A short distance further his slide is suddenly terminated by a wooden fence post!

This accident could have been avoided if the walker had carried an ice axe and had learned some basic winter skills, the most important of which is self-arrest, commonly known as the ice-axe brake. *This is described in more detail on page 104.*

We are not concerned here with technical ice climbing which requires specialist equipment, but with more general winter walking and mountain-eering which may include simple gully climbs. A typical example of the type of ice axe required for this type of activity is shown in *figure 2*. It should have a curved pick with a serrated underside and a sharp, chisel end, and a wide, straight-edged, flat-ended adze which mirrors the curve of the pick. The head (the pick and adze together) will generally be forged from a single piece of metal, and it is useful if this has a karabiner hole drilled through it at the top end of the shaft.

The curve of the head should approximate to the circumference of the swing of the axe when held towards the base of the shaft. The shaft itself should be straight with an oval rather than round cross-section, and traditional wooden shafts (usually of straight grained hickory) have now largely been replaced by stronger alloy or reinforced fibreglass, covered with a plastic or synthetic rubber material which affords good grip even when you are wearing gloves or mittens. The shaft should terminate in a sharp spike.

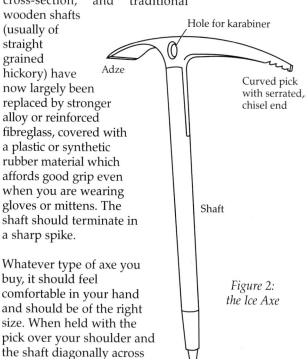

Figure 2:
the Ice Axe

Whatever type of axe you buy, it should feel comfortable in your hand and should be of the right size. When held with the pick over your shoulder and the shaft diagonally across your chest, the end of the shaft should protrude slightly below your hip. This is a good general length. If you intend to use it only for walking, the shaft can be slightly longer; if you intend to do a fair amount of easy gully work, the shaft can be slightly shorter. Many axes come with some form of wrist loop. This often takes the form of a short sling attached to a ring which can slide along the length of the shaft, although longer slings attached through the hole in the head of the axe are almost as common. Whatever the type, the sling should be large enough for you to put a mittened hand through comfortably, but should also have some form of slider or tensioning device so that the sling can be tightened around the wrist.

Although, at first glance, it may seem sensible to wear such a wrist loop (indeed, it is indispensable when climbing), it can lead to several complications when walking.

Firstly, *(as described on page 104)* when traversing snow slopes the axe should always be held in the upslope hand. This means when zig-zagging up a slope you should be able to move your axe freely from hand to hand (there are similar considerations when step cutting). Many people dispense with the wrist loop in these situations. Secondly, if an attempted self arrest is unsuccessful (even in a practice situation), the ice axe which is attached to you via a wrist loop can do you more damage than the fall itself! When not in use the wrist loop should either be removed altogether (simple on some axes, impossible on others) or wrapped around the head and secured in place so that it does not flap around or drag along the ground where it may get caught in crampons.

Once you have bought your axe you need to look after it. Make sure you keep the pick, adze and spike sharp and free from rust, and buy rubber protectors for both the head and the spike (essential if taking it on public transport).

*Information on how to carry, hold and use an ice axe is given in section 3.*

## Crampons

Modern crampons come in all sorts of shapes and sizes, some of which are hi-tech items of equipment designed for modern technical ice climbing and therefore totally unsuitable for more general winter walking and simple snow gully climbing. *Crampon technique and the major pitfalls are mentioned in section 3.* Here we are concerned only with crampon types.

At the bottom end of the scale come lightweight instep crampons which can be quickly and easily fitted and removed from the boot. As their name implies, they sit between the front of the heel and the backmost tread of the front part of the sole, and should be a snug fit. While they may be useful to give added security across short sections of ice on low-level or valley walks, they are totally unsuitable for general purpose winter walking and climbing. Even if you intend to keep well away from steep ground and gullies, instep crampons should not be seen as a substitute for full crampons.

Next come flexible crampons. These come in a variety of designs, some of which have eight points, others of which have ten, but all are based on a central springy metal plate. In some designs the front two points point forward at an angle of about 45°. The method of attachment to the boot (which, as we will see, is critical) often leaves much to be desired, being done via one long strap and four attachment points. As with instep crampons, these may be useful for short sections of ice on low level walks, but they are totally unsuitable for general use in the mountains.

At the opposite end of the scale come technical ice-climbing crampons. These are usually totally rigid and come with a wide variety of point shapes and sizes. They are not suitable for general mountain use and fall way outside the scope of this book. The most suitable general purpose crampons should have ten downward-facing points and two horizontal forward-facing points which should be angled slightly downwards, either flat or curved. The front two downward-facing points should also be inclined slightly forwards.

These crampons can be thought of as being divided into two sections, the four rear points making up one, and the eight front points making up the other. These sections are connected by a metal plate which effectively forms a hinge below the instep of the boot. This hinge is vital for without it the crampons would soon fail due to constant flexing. This is especially true if you wear boots which are either not fully stiffened or which do not have a totally flat sole.

The fit of the crampon on the boot is especially important. Indeed, the crampons should fit so well that they remain on the boot without any form of binding. Few crampons are totally adjustable throughout a range of sizes, so it is important to take your boots with you when you go to buy. It is usually necessary to match crampons to boots. Things to watch for are the position of the inside point (which can be fouled by the instep of the boot), and the position of the front points relative to the toe of the boot. When a straight edge is placed across the front of the boot there should be about 2cms of front point sticking out. It may also be necessary to fit a heel bar to prevent the boot from slipping backwards. Once fitted, make sure any screws, bolts or nuts are fully tightened. It is prudent to use a proprietary locking agent to reduce the chance of them loosening accidentally.

When you come to wear your crampons, place them on the ground with all rings and straps outside the framework, clear any snow from the sole of your boot, then step into them from a standing position, making sure the boot sits firmly on the frame. There are two main methods of attachment, these being straps (either traditional or French-style) and clip-on bindings. As with fit, the method of attachment is crucial and I recommend you visit your local friendly retailer and ask advice. The best all-round method is traditional straps. These are flexible in use and easy to adjust and tension.

Make sure all straps are fastened neatly and without twists into the correct buckle. Fasten the back strap first, guiding it right around the ankle well below the ankle cuff of the boot before doing up the buckle. Now secure the front straps, threading them in the correct direction and order through the rings (see figure 3). French-style straps make use of a fixed strap with a ring at the front end of the boot. Although apparently more simple,

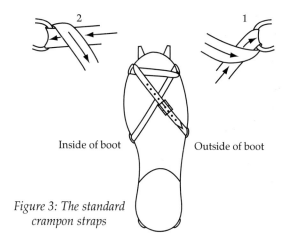

Inside of boot          Outside of boot

*Figure 3: The standard crampon straps*

they are not so flexible and can be difficult to tension correctly. The back strap is secured first (as per traditional straps), then the front strap is passed through the toe ring (which must be in precisely the correct position) and secured.

No matter which strap method is chosen, the straps themselves should be made from neoprene-coated nylon with pin-type buckles, and should be checked on a regular basis. These should be pulled as tight as comfort allows with the proviso that there should be no restriction of circulation to the toes. Once secured, the strap protruding from the buckles should neither be too long nor too short – about 4-5cms is ideal. It is prudent to connect the straps to the crampons with two sets of rivets.

Clip-on bindings (crampons with this type of binding are sometimes called step-in crampons) are the quickest and easiest method of attaching crampons to boots, and have largely replaced straps. However, they are generally only suitable for use on good quality plastic boots because the attachment is via the welt. This is often narrower on leather boots, and prone to wear, so may not afford a positive grip.

In use, the toe of the boot is first placed under the front bail, then the tensioning lever is placed on the rear welt and pulled up to the back of the boot. It is then secured in place by means of a strap. This strap is often of nylon webbing, in which case it should be done up via two D-rings rather than a spring buckle. This method is far less likely to slip, but can be difficult to undo. The front bail, tensioning lever and cables, and restraining strap should be inspected on a regular basis for signs of wear.

Crampon points should be kept sharp using a hand-held file rather than a grinding tool as the heat may affect the temper of the metal. Front points should be sharpened from the top in a for-wards direction; other points should be sharpened along their edges. Regular checks should also be made on all nuts, bolts and screws, and any areas of possible metal fatigue such as hinges and posts.

## Snow goggles

In winter conditions when there is continuous snow cover, snow blindness is a hazard – even on a cloudy day. You should therefore have with you a pair of snow goggles, preferably with good ultra-violet and infra-red filter lenses. Ordinary sun glasses are not suitable, no matter how effective the lenses, because they do not give protection to the side of the eyes. If you find goggles too claustrophobic, glacier glasses, again with filtering lenses are a good alternative, so long as they have effective side shields.

## Sleeping bags and bivi-bags

In winter conditions, especially in the Scottish Highlands or any remote site, at least one member of the party (if not everyone) should carry a good quality, 4-season sleeping bag. This may make the difference between life or death in an emergency. If this is combined with a breathable-fabric bivi-bag, so much the better.

## Helmets

Many accidents in the mountains involve head injuries and you would be wise to consider carefully whether you need a helmet. Situations where it would be prudent for you to wear them include scrambling and general winter mountaineering in easy snow gullies. Should you intend to become involved in more serious rock, snow or ice climbing on mountain crags they should be regarded as an essential item of equipment.

Two main types of helmet are available, one made from fibreglass (GRP), the other plastic. Both give protection but in a slightly different way. Both should be discarded after suffering any severe impact. Whatever the type chosen it should be reasonably light and fairly compact, and should not restrict the vision. It should also be comfortable. Those which give some protection to the temples are safer than those that do not, but are often less comfortable. The cradle should be adjustable to allow for the wearing of a hat, and the chin strap should be easily adjustable and connected via Y-straps to give stability.

## Ropes and ancillaries

Although technical rock climbing and snow/ice climbing are beyond the scope of this book, there are times when a rope should be regarded as an essential item of equipment. This is particularly the case in scrambling and winter walking where simple snow gullies are likely to be encountered. The rope best suited to these situations is of Kernmantle construction, having a core of lightly twisted nylon strands held together with a plaited nylon sheath. It should have a diameter of between 9mm and 11mm, 9mm being the more popular for scrambling because it is lighter. The length of rope required will depend very much upon the situation in which it is to be used, but generally speaking a length of between 30m and 45m will be adequate.

It is essential that only rope designed for rock climbing and mountaineering is used, and that it should be dynamic. This means that it will stretch slightly under load, thus absorbing some of the shock of a fall. Static or prestretched ropes are totally unsuitable and should not be used. Make sure that your rope comes from a recognised manufacturer and has UIAA approval.

Ropes should be stored either loosely coiled or

(better) laced in a cool, dry, airy environment, well away from sources of heat or contamination. If they get wet, they should be allowed to dry naturally. If they get dirty they should be washed in cold, clean, preferably running water. Battery acid, petrol and mineral oils, in particular, are seriously detrimental, so bear this in mind when slinging the rope in the boot of your car. *Methods of coiling are discussed on page 81.*

Ropes generally have a lifespan of not more than three years under normal usage, owing as much to the effects of ultraviolet light as to fair wear and tear. However, this can be seriously reduced under certain circumstances, and you should get into the habit of checking your rope for signs of wear or damage every time you handle it. Things to look for include excessive fluffing of the sheath, and any distortion of the core. Suspect ropes should be destroyed. Avoid treading on the rope as this can cause indirect damage by forcing grit particles into the core as well as direct damage if it is lying over a sharp stone. Beware securing the rope in such a way that it runs or rubs over sharp edges, or allowing a loaded rope to rub across rough rock.

Although you should be able to make use of the rope alone, there are a couple of other things which will make your life easier. Tape slings made from nylon webbing can be useful in a variety of situations. Although it is possible to buy webbing off the reel and tie the loops yourself using a tape knot, the best and most convenient slings are ready sewn slings made from full-weight 25mm wide webbing. These come in a variety of sizes, 240cms being the most versatile. Two or three slings should suffice for most situations. You should store and look after slings in exactly the same way as ropes.

To go with each of your slings you will need a screwgate karabiner. Like your rope, this should be UIAA approved. Offset D or HMS (pear shape) designs are the most practical as they allow the use of friction hitches *(see page 88)*. Alloy karabiners are the norm as they are light in weight. However, they wear quickly if used with dirty ropes and should be discarded if dropped onto rock from heights of more than about 5m. Steel karabiners are much heavier but resist wear far better. Karabiners need very little maintenance apart from an occasional light spray with WD40 or (better) a silicon lubricant, paying particular attention to the hinge, screwgate and spring. Wipe away any excess.

## Other useful items

There are several other bits and pieces which can go a long way towards making your mountain journeys more comfortable. Some are essential in certain conditions, and in this category I would include sun-screen, sun glasses, and insect repellent. No matter what the conditions or time of year, a short length of paracord can have many uses including emergency repairs to rucksack or gaiters, and spare bootlace. A plastic bag containing a few sheets of toilet tissue can also be useful.

Some form of sit mat may make breaks more comfortable and can easily be carried down the back of the daysack where it will provide extra padding. This is best formed from an offcut of closed-cell foam such as a sleepmat. Some experienced walkers never venture into the hills without their binoculars or camera. Others take books to help them identify birds, plants or rocks, or paper and pencil to draw or note down things they have seen. In the final analysis, only you can decide what you wish to carry. So long as you have the basic essentials, it really is up to you. Indeed, some experienced mountaineers may be appalled that I have neglected to mention some piece of equipment which they feel is vital. If this is the case, write and tell me, make your case, and I may include it in any future edition!

# 3    Hill walking skills

I have a pet theory that most people have forgotten the correct way to walk. We spend so much of our time on level pavements, carpeted floors, ramps and stairs that our bodies are unused to moving along rough paths and across trackless terrain. The result is that not only do we place our feet incorrectly, we also hold our bodies in the wrong position relative to our feet and the ground.

This section looks at a range of hillwalking skills, both basic movement skills and more specialised safety techniques. I must emphasise that these skills cannot be learned from a book. Proficiency will only come with practice and experience. I encourage you to practise all the skills, but in particular you should gain practical experience of ropework techniques and winter skills (especially the ice axe arrest) in a safe environment before you need them in an emergency. When things go wrong in the mountains, they tend to do so with alarming speed and severity. It is of little use referring to a book at the time – the techniques should already be ingrained by practice and experience so that they have become almost second nature.

## Pace

The basic mountain walking technique is a regular, rhythmic pace. This is a major factor in the safe enjoyment of mountain walking. Although there will be days when it feels good to stride out, and others when you gain pleasure from dawdling, you should generally aim to walk at a steady pace with a medium stride which uses the least amount of energy. Once you have found your rhythm and got into your stride, your body takes over leaving the mind to do other things – including enjoying the surroundings. This rhythm should be maintained up hill and down dale. If you wish to speed up or slow down, you do so by altering the length of stride, not the pace or the rhythm.

Most experienced mountaineers finish the day at the same pace as they started; they have what could be termed a 24-hour pace which can be kept up almost indefinitely. So avoid the temptation to rush off at the start, no matter how much energy you may have – you never know when you may need reserves!

Deliberate, precise foot placement is paramount, especially over rough or loose terrain. Indeed, no matter what the surface, place each foot carefully, with as much of the sole of the boot on the ground as possible. Choose the easiest route, avoiding, where possible, high steps and long strides. When the terrain becomes rougher or more difficult, shorten your stride so you can maintain your rhythm. Whatever the conditions underfoot, try to keep the body-weight over the feet so that all the work of walking is done with the strong thigh and stomach muscles.

Good route selection should be on two levels. Not only should you look ahead so as to choose the easiest line through the landscape, but you should also look closer to hand in order to plan precisely where each foot is going to be placed.

## Security on steep ground

As the ground becomes steeper, so route selection, foot placement and body position become increasingly important. When going uphill, shorten the stride, flex the ankles so that feet can be kept flat to the slope, and lock each leg at the knee as you step up. If the ground is loose or slippery, try to place your feet in such a way that there is something against them (such as a protruding stone) which will prevent them from slipping downslope, even if this means turning your feet sideways. Keep your body upright with you weight over your feet, and try to avoid springing up from your toes. Every upward step you take should be powered by your thigh and stomach muscles.

As the ground steepens still further you will probably find it easier to zig-zag in an ascending traverse, moving diagonally backwards and forwards across the slope. Indeed, many of the older mountain paths (such as those made by shepherds, drovers and miners) do this. If the terrain is trackless, the length and angle of each zig and zag should be determined by the nature of the terrain (and personal preference). Resist the temptation to edge your boots. Instead, flex your ankles and keep the soles of your feet flat to the slope. Few slopes other than rock slabs are perfectly smooth, and you should take advantage of the natural bulges and indentations. Plan your route in almost microscopic detail. Look first for flatter areas where you can safely place both feet prior to changing direction, then connect these with lines of weakness containing lumps, bumps and places where local projections create small platforms from which it is difficult for your foot to slip.

Although it seems the natural thing to do, try to guard against leaning in to the slope. If my experience on courses is anything to go by, some people find this incredibly difficult to do the first few times, so you may have to make a conscious effort. Remember, your body should remain upright with the weight over your feet. This is especially important if the ground is loose or wet. If you lean in, your alter your centre of gravity and place an outward pressure on your feet making them far more likely to slip *(see figure 4)*. If there is a drop below you, the temptation is to pull yourself into the slope with your hands whereas, in reality, the safest thing to do is to push yourself away from the slope with your hands!

Many people find going downhill harder than going up. As with ascent, you should shorten your stride and flex your ankles to keep your feet flat to the slope, and make use of the local topography to help keep your feet from slipping. The smaller the step, the less of a shock load comes onto the foot, and the less likely you are to slip. Resist the temptation to lean back or dig in your heels, especially if your are wearing boots with cut-away soles *(see page 43)*. Unlike ascent, however, where the knees should be locked, it is better to keep each leg very slightly bent so that the shock of the

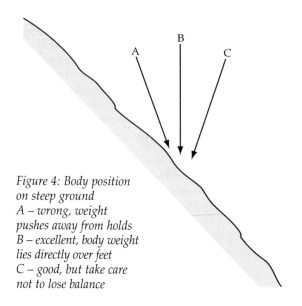

Figure 4: Body position
on steep ground
A – wrong, weight
pushes away from holds
B – excellent, body weight
lies directly over feet
C – good, but take care
not to lose balance

descent is taken and absorbed by the thigh muscles
rather than the cartilage. No matter whether going
up or down, the body weight should be kept as
near vertical as possible so that it acts directly
down on the legs and feet.

Few mountain slopes are at a constant angle, and
you should be aware of two particular types of
slope. Convex slopes are those which begin
gradually and become steeper as they descend.
Conversely, concave slopes start off steeply and
become less steep as they descend. Particularly
when you are on unfamiliar terrain (and especially
in poor visibility), you should aim to descend

concave slopes rather than convex ones. This is simply because you can always see what is ahead of you when descending a concave slope, whereas the future is hidden when descending a convex slope.

Of course, in practice, many mountain slopes are complex slopes, with areas of concavity and areas of convexity. When descending this type of terrain, use your map interpretation skills to search out the concave areas and descend these, even if you have to weave your way backwards and forwards across the mountainside.

On slopes where there are loose boulders around, be aware of other walkers around you in case they dislodge a stone. If you, yourself, accidentally dislodge a stone which starts to roll or bounce downslope, bellow 'below' at the top of your voice, even if you cannot see anyone *(see also page 97)*.

## Scrambling

A vast hazy area sandwiched between adventurous walking and technical rock climbing, scrambling is potentially the most dangerous activity in the mountains, yet it is one of the most rewarding. This is probably more than just coincidence! A good maxim for anyone going scrambling is 'discretion is the better part of valour'. Indeed, I frequently tell clients on scrambling courses that I live my life by the rule 'Bottle out and run away; live to climb another day!', and there is more than a small degree of truth in this.

If I were to discuss fully the skills of scrambling, I

would need to use the whole of this book. All I can do here is give you some pointers and mention a few basic skills. I consider the most important skill of scrambling to be the ability to relax. Indeed, when scrambling your moves should be made as much with your mind as with your body. My justification for this is simple. If I were to place a paving slab on the floor, virtually everyone could stand on it on one leg and hop. However, if I were to place the same paving slab on top of a pillar five metres high, most of those selfsame people would be unable to do it. Physically we can do it; mentally, we cannot.

In basic terms, the movement techniques in scrambling are simply an extension of the steep ground skills discussed earlier: body upright, weight over the feet, resist the temptation to lean in. Route finding and route selection become even more important. Indeed, finding and planning your route calls for good judgement, and that you can only learn through experience. In order to prevent yourself from scrambling into difficulty, not only do you need to work out your general line of ascent, you also need to work out each individual move as far in advance as you can. You need to learn to read the rock, and many newcomers to scrambling get themselves into difficulties simply because they look only at the rock in front of them instead of the rock all around them.

Moreover, you should never climb up something you cannot climb down. I advise you to practise downclimbing because it does not come naturally and most people find it far harder than climbing up. If you are really keen to try scrambling, my advice is to go initially with a more experienced companion or book on a scrambling course at a reputable centre. If you want to get the most from such a course, the client:instructor ratio should not exceed 3:1. If you have already been scrambling a little and want to learn more, it would be useful to try some basic rock climbing, again either with an experienced companion or with a good centre.

In terms of equipment, you need very little apart from your basic hill kit. However, you should note that your boots need to be somewhat more sturdy than lightweight summer walking boots. Moreover, particularly on the more difficult scrambles (grade 2 and above), it would be prudent to wear a helmet and to carry a rope and perhaps a couple of tape slings with screwgate karabiners. Of course, it is of little use carrying this gear if you do not know how to use it correctly.

## Basic ropework

The type of rope suitable for use in scrambling has already been discussed in section 2. In this part of the book we are going to look at a few simple ways in which it can be used. In order to use your rope safely and effectively in all situations, you need to be proficient in a number of skills, these being rope management, tying on, locating and using anchors, belaying, and abseiling. You should also be able to tie a number of specific knots quickly and effectively (no matter what the weather is doing nor how cold your hands), and should know which knot is appropriate to a given circumstance. Again I

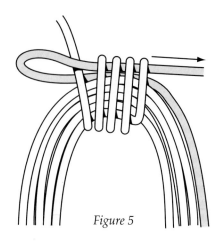

*Figure 5*

must stress that these skills cannot be learned from a book. You should practise them in a safe environment before you need to use them for real.

When handled correctly, your rope can be a real friend. If mishandled, mistreated or used without circumspection, it can precipitate your downfall with potentially fatal results. Basic rope management skills are therefore essential.

Ropes can be coiled in one of three ways, each of which has advantages and disadvantages. The mountaineer's coil *(see figure 5)* used to be the standard way to coil and carry a rope and is still commonly seen. With practice it can be done quickly and neatly, and if you make each coil from a length of rope the width of your extended arms, the coil will sit comfortably around your neck and over one shoulder. However, in order to get each coil to sit flat against its neighbours, it is necessary to twist the rope with the result that there is a danger it can kink in use. This is particularly true if you store your rope coiled in this way. When uncoiling, undo the lashing then remove each coil in order, letting the rope fall to the ground in loose loops.

The butterfly coil *(see figure 6)* is quick and easy and has much to recommend it. It can be done with the rope doubled or single. If using it doubled, first find the middle of the rope and then put the two sides around your neck in such a way that you can place your thumb through the mid-point with your arm extended down your side. If using it with a single rope, place it around your neck so that one end touches the ground. Coils of equal

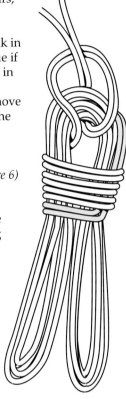

*Figure 6: tying off the Alpine butterfly coil*

length can quickly be made by passing the rope backwards and forwards across the back of the neck and running it around the thumb. The advantage of this method is that it is unnecessary to twist the rope to form the coils, so there is less chance of the rope kinking in use. When the coils are secured in the way shown, the rope can easily be carried like a rucksack, the ends being tied around your waist, thus securing the coils. Ropes coiled this way should be uncoiled as per the mountaineer's coil.

Dutch lacing is a coiling technique borrowed from cavers. In this method the rope is first quartered by holding both ends together then, without letting go of the ends, running the rope through your hands until you find the middle. Now tie an overhand slip knot using all four strands, and pass a loop of the quartered rope through this to form another loop. Continue in this way until all the rope has been chained, passing the ends through the final loop to secure it. There is no need to pull the loops tight. This is the ideal method of coiling to use to store a rope. When uncoiling, pull the ends out of the final loop and the whole rope will unravel with ease. However, as the rope will still be quartered at this point, it will be necessary to run it through your hands twice before you can use it without risk of tangles.

No matter which method you use, make sure when uncoiling that you throw the first end away to one side so that the coils following it do not hide it. This first end becomes the bottom end of the rope (because it leads to the bottom of the pile of coils). The end which you finish with becomes the top end of the rope (because it leads to the top of the pile of coils). Whenever you use it, you should always take rope from the top end or else you run the danger of tangles.

In order to explain the other techniques in what is hopefully a clear and concise way, I am going to use a scenario. Imagine that you are with a companion at the bottom of a short rock step. You have decided that you can scramble up it without too much difficulty, but your companion is not so sure of his own abilities and has asked you to protect him with the rope. You have uncoiled the rope into loose loops on the ground where it will not be trodden on. The next thing you need to do is tie on.

There are two methods of tying on to the rope – the waist line and the harness. The waist line is formed simply by passing the rope around your waist and securing it with a bowline *(figure 7)*.

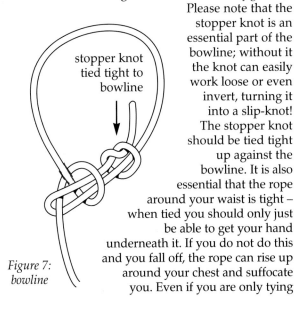

stopper knot
tied tight to
bowline

*Figure 7: bowline*

Please note that the stopper knot is an essential part of the bowline; without it the knot can easily work loose or even invert, turning it into a slip-knot! The stopper knot should be tied tight up against the bowline. It is also essential that the rope around your waist is tight – when tied you should only just be able to get your hand underneath it. If you do not do this and you fall off, the rope can rise up around your chest and suffocate you. Even if you are only tying on to belay someone, the rope should still be tied tight to prevent the risk of excessive movement. Although this is a quick and simple way of tying on, please note that this method is not recommended for lowering nor for use in any situation where immediate recovery from a fall is unlikely, because of the risk of suffocation through compression of the diaphragm. Under these circumstances, or when dealing with children, very nervous or heavy adults, some form of harness is preferable.

This is most easily tied using a Thompson knot *(figure 8)*. Because this is being used to form a harness, it should be tied to the right size. When forming the four loops, size them against the person who will wear the harness, the correct length being either 'nose-to-toes' (from the end of the nose when looking down to the top of the boot) or 'neck-to-deck' (from the top of the sternum to the ground), whichever you prefer. Tie the overhand knot in the middle of the loops

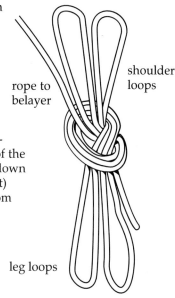

rope to belayer

shoulder loops

leg loops

*Figure 8: Thompson knot*

initially, but make adjustments later to ensure that the harness fits properly.

In the scenario given, you now make your way carefully to the top of the rock step, your companion ensuring that the rope pays out freely. If there is any risk that you may fall, you should choose another route. If, for some reason, this is impossible, your companion should belay you using one of the methods described below.

Obviously there will be no rope above you, so if you fall you are almost certain to hit the ground unless you can find a suitable flake of rock behind which you can pass the rope. In the event of a fall this acts as a running belay which may prevent you from hitting the ground. Running belays can also be formed by passing tape slings over projections or around chockstones then passing the climbing rope through a karabiner attached to it. Ideally your companion should be tied to anchors which will resist a pull in any direction *(see below)*.

On reaching the top you must search for some form of anchor. Typical anchors include flakes of rock, large boulders, and chockstones jammed firmly in cracks, but choosing a suitable anchor or combination of anchors requires practice and careful thought. Whatever you use it should obviously be solid. Kick it, pull it, try to destroy it. If it moves, avoid it! You are going to use the anchor to secure the rope in one of two ways. Think about the direction in which any pull will come in the event that your companion falls, and try to work out what will happen not only to the anchor, but to anything attached to it. If, for example, there is any danger that a rope tied around it could pull off under load, or could run over a sharp edge, look again. Try, also, to find an anchor which lies in such a position that, when in use, you can see your companion.

Anchors can be used in one of two ways: either directly as a means of securing the rope in order to hold a fall, or indirectly as a means of securing you so that you can hold a fall. The technique of holding the rope in order to prevent a slip from becoming a fall is known as belaying.

The quickest, simplest and most straightforward way of belaying is the direct belay. In this method the rope is passed directly around the anchor, the anchor providing sufficient friction to aid you in arresting the fall. As the climber ascends, so the rope is kept taught by being pulled around the anchor. In order to be effective, the anchor should be fairly broad, and should have no sharp edges which could cut the rope. Additionally, the rope between the anchor and the climber (the live rope) should run straight. If additional friction is required you can use a body belay as described below. The anchor must obviously be bombproof! If it is not and it fails, you have no hope at all of stopping the fall, and if you are using a body belay, you could be pulled over the edge as well.

If you are carrying a tape sling and karabiner, there is an alternative and arguably safer method of using the direct belay. In this method the sling is passed around the anchor and the rope is placed in

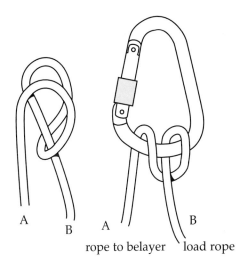

A  B  A    B

rope to belayer  load rope

*Figure 9: Italian Hitch*

the karabiner using an Italian Hitch *(figure 9)*. It is important that the live rope is located on the back-bar side of the karabiner and not on the gate side.

To use this method correctly, you must stand in front of the knot and guide the live rope into the karabiner whilst pulling the slack through with the other hand. In the event of a slip, pulling on the slack rope (the rope between the anchor and you) will cause the knot to bite thus arresting a fall, so although you can let go of the live rope, you should always have one hand firmly grasping the slack rope. Because the Italian Hitch is reversible (i.e. it provides friction both when taking in the rope and when paying it out), this method of belaying is particularly useful in an emergency when, for example, lowering an injured person down a short rock step.

There are times when a direct belay may be inappropriate, such as when the anchors are not quite as solid as could be wished for, when they are situated some way from the edge of the rock step, or when no single anchor lies in exactly the right position to allow the rope to run in a straight line to the climber. Under such circumstances, an indirect belay may well be a better option. In this method, you secure yourself to the anchor then pass the rope around your body (a body belay) in such a way that you can arrest a fall.

To connect yourself to the anchor, take the rope issuing from the bowline around your waist and pass it either around the anchor or through a karabiner attached to a sling passing around the anchor. Stand at the point from which you will be belaying *(see below)* and thread a loop of the rope coming back from the anchor, through your waistline, pull it tight, and secure it using a figure of eight knot *(see figure 10)*.

If you feel it would be prudent to back up this single anchor with another, or if a line drawn between you, the anchor and the climber is not straight, tie into further anchors using the same method. When using two or more anchors your safe area lies anywhere within the angle formed by the outside anchors. Certain factors must be considered regarding the relationship between the position of the anchors, the position in which you stand (the

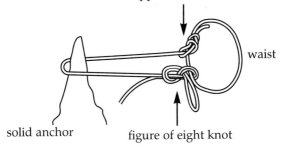

bowline with stopper knot tied to the knot

waist

solid anchor

figure of eight knot

*Figure 10: Tying in to an anchor using a figure of eight knot around the waist*

stance) and the route to be taken by the climber.

Firstly, when standing at the stance, all the ropes between you and the anchors should be taut. Indeed, you should be leaning against them. You should be facing out with the anchors behind you, so the knots tied around your waistline should also be behind you – in line with the respective anchors. If this is not done you could be pulled over the edge of the rock step if your companion falls.

Secondly, the direction of pull which will act on you in the event of any fall should pass directly to the anchors. If using multiple anchors, you should be standing within the safe area; if using only one anchor, your stance should lie on a straight line drawn between the anchor and the climber.

Thirdly, as the direction of pull on you in this

scenario is going to be downwards, your anchors should ideally be above you. This is particularly important if the anchors are within 1 or 2 metres of the stance.

Once you have secured yourself to the anchors, get comfortable on the stance and pull in all the slack rope which lies between you and your companion. When it comes tight, pass it over your head and shoulders so you can run it around your waist. It should lie above the lines running from you to your anchors. Identify the two parts of the rope: the live rope (running from you to the climber), and the slack rope. Take a twist in the slack rope, passing it over and around your forearm before holding it. Brace yourself by leaning forward on your anchor lines, standing with your legs slightly apart and with the foot on the same side as the live rope slightly forward, knee braced. This is the basic position for the body belay.

To take the rope in, hold both live and slack ropes with your live hand, slide the slack hand back to your hips, grasp the rope firmly and pull it forward, feeding it into the live hand (figure 11). To give out slack rope, slide the slack hand forward then feed the rope around the waist with the live hand whilst moving the slack hand back towards your hips. To lock off in the event of a fall, bring your slack hand smartly across your chest. All this takes practice!

There may be times when, for one reason or another, you are unable to see or hear your companion clearly, and yet precise instructions and a

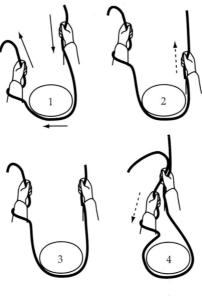

——► Hands gripping, rope moving
----► Hands gliding, rope stationary

*Figure 11: The body belay. This illustrates the sequence of moves when taking in the rope. The slack hand is on the left of all four diagrams*

knowledge of exactly what each other is doing at any given time are vital for safety. You therefore need to be able to communicate with clarity and without ambiguity.

When climbing up and being belayed, let your companion know if you are using a running belay by calling 'runner on'. This will alert him to the fact that if you fall, the rope may now pull upwards instead of downwards. You should remain on belay until you have tied yourself in to your anchors at the top, at which point you call 'safe'. You now need to take in all the slack rope, so call 'taking in' and continue pulling until your companion calls 'that's me' to indicate that the rope is now tight on him.

Once you have secured the rope in either a direct or indirect belay, and are in a position to arrest a fall, invite your companion to climb by calling 'climb when you're ready'. He should acknowledge your call by shouting 'climbing', but should not start climbing until you have replied 'okay'. If he starts to climb before this and you have not heard him, he will hit the ground if he falls off.

Whilst on the rock face only two calls should be used, although it is common to hear several more if the climber gets into difficulties! If, for some reason, the climber wants to descend, he should call 'slack'. When you hear this call, do not suddenly give him three metres of rope – simply allow the rope to run out as it is needed. If, on the other hand, there seems to be too much slack rope and the climber wants it tightened, he should call 'take in'. Never mix the two by shouting 'take in the slack'. This can lead to obvious confusion.

The final ropework technique that needs to be mentioned is abseiling – a method of descending a rope in a controlled manner. It is fair to say that many accidents are caused by the misuse of this technique so it should not be approached lightly.

The basic idea is to find the middle of the rope and loop this around a bombproof anchor, the two halves then being dropped down the rock step to be descended. If the anchor is chosen with care, the rope can then be retrieved once the descent has been made simply by pulling on one end.

There are two methods of abseiling which are applicable to a scrambling or hill-walking situation. In the classic abseil the double rope from the anchor is passed between your legs, around the back of one thigh, across your chest and over the shoulder opposite the thigh. It is then passed across your back and is held firmly in the hand on the same side as the thigh around which it passes (*figure 12*). You will not want to go fast if you use this technique! In the sling-assisted classic a tape sling is formed into a sit harness. To do this, hold the sling so that the stitched join is against the small of your back and the karabiner hangs down

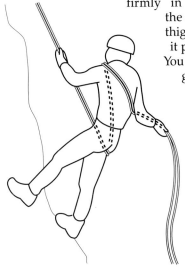

*Figure 12: Classic abseil*

between your legs. Bring the two sides around your sides then pull the karabiner between your legs and clip it into the two side loops *(figure 13)*. There should be three loops in the karabiner, and the tape around your back should sit above your hips. Stand facing the anchor and pass the double rope over one shoulder. Pull it down and clip it into the karabiner and do up the screwgate. Now pass the rope

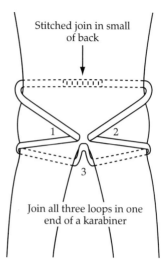

Figure 13: Sit harness formed from a tape sling (viewed from the front)

from your shoulder across your back so you can hold it firmly in the opposite hand.

To descend, stand with your back to the cliff and walk backwards to the edge, allowing the rope to slide around your body and through your hand in a controlled manner. One hand will be holding the rope which goes across your back, the other should be holding the rope coming from the anchor. Resist the temptation to hold your weight with the anchormost hand – it is the backmost hand which controls the abseil and holds your weight. When you get to the edge, slowly lean backwards until you are at an angle of between 60-80 degrees to the rock. Keep your legs fairly straight, pushing away from the rock, and your feet as flat to the rock as possible, with your heels well down. Turn slightly sideways with the controlling hand lowermost, and carefully walk backwards down the rockface. As with the belaying techniques, this requires practice, and should preferably be done in a supervised, non-hazardous environment before it needs to be used in an emergency.

If you would like to know more about ropework or to learn how to use the techniques correctly, safely and effectively, I recommend you ask a more experienced companion to show you the ropes (sorry!) or join a suitable course at a reputable centre.

## Moving on scree

Ascending scree can be laborious, and should be avoided wherever possible. However, there will be times when it is necessary. The same movement skills apply here as in other steep ground situations: move slowly and steadily, taking small paces and placing your feet carefully and with precision. If there are several in the party, it is advisable to ascend in a line abreast or an arrowhead formation. In this way the risk of someone being hit by dislodged material is minimised. If you do dislodge something and it gathers momentum, shout the warning 'Below!'.

If the scree is steep or long and you wish to zig-zag,

keep the party fairly close together, and be aware of people who are zigging when you are zagging! Not only should you be conscious of people below you upon whom rocks may fall, you should also be conscious of people above you who could dislodge something onto you.

Descending scree is best done in a steady, controlled manner. Again, be aware of the danger of falling material and adopt an arrowhead formation if appropriate. Scree running can be exhilarating, but it can also be extremely dangerous. It will also damage both your boots and the environment. Indeed, several of the classic scree runs are now unrunnable because most of the loose material has gone. The basic technique involves taking large steps down the scree, digging the heels well back. As the stones begin to move, go with them, taking large steps as if walking down an escalator. It is possible to gain considerable momentum, your speed being equal to that of your pace plus that of the falling stones! When you want to stop, take a little jump and dig both heels well back. As with all other movement on steep ground, try to keep upright. If you lean back your feet will fly out from under you and you will end up sitting down but still moving (not a pleasant experience). If you lean too far forward you run the risk of somersaulting headfirst down the slope.

Before running down any scree there are a number of factors you should consider. Firstly, it is important that you are absolutely certain that you can see all of the slope. This will be impossible if the visibility is poor or if it is nearing dusk. Secondly, it is very easy for small drops to be camouflaged by the similarity in the stones above and below them, and it is therefore unwise to run down any scree slope which you have not previously viewed from below. Thirdly, the slope should be composed of boulders which are fairly small and uniform in size. Avoid slopes where there are large islands of rock or large boulders perched on the scree.

Scree often issues from gullies. These can be really nasty areas, damp and greasy, containing much loose material. When moving through gullies, either in ascent or descent, it is best to keep close together so any dislodged material can be palmed from person to person before it has a chance of gathering momentum. Obviously, if the gully is only short, it is safest and most convenient for people to ascend it one at a time, but it may be possible to divide larger gullies into sections between large rock steps which offer shelter from falling material. If this can be done, the party can move one at a time between these safer areas.

## Winter skills

First and foremost we need to dispel a few misconceptions and put things into perspective. It is true to say that you can walk safely in the winter hills without crampons whereas you cannot do so without an ice axe. Although good crampon technique can, in most circumstances, reduce the need to cut steps, thus speeding things up (an important consideration), crampons themselves bring with them their own particular set of hazards. Indeed, crampons can be extremely dangerous pieces of equipment because they can lull the inexperienced wearer into a false sense of security, giving a feeling of invulnerability out of all proportion to the extra safety they can give. Make no mistake about it, to venture into the mountains without an ice axe when there is snow on the ground is nothing short of madness. However, it is of little use taking an ice axe if you do not know how to use it correctly. Despite what you may have heard to the contrary, the most important use of your ice axe is not cutting steps, but self arrest *(see below)*. It is a sad but demonstrable fact that the vast majority of winter accidents are caused by simple slips on easy ground.

Most people are familiar with the soft, white fluffy stuff which lies in the back garden in winter. However, this fun eliciting, snowball material is only one type of snow. During a day trip in the mountains you might start on soft, wet snow which compacts in the cleats of your boots forming blocks of ice, wander into an area of deepening powder through which you wade literally waist deep, then come to a slope where a thin crust of windslab supports your weight for a few steps before giving way and plunging you knee deep into the powder below. You can have snow the consistency of modelling clay in which you can kick solid steps, and snow which has consolidated to such an extent that a heavy kick will only make a slight indentation.

Step kicking is an art. Although hard work, it should appear virtually effortless, and good technique will result in less energy being used – an important consideration when on a strenuous outing. The basic technique is to hold the body upright and swing your leg from the knee letting momentum and weight do most of the work. Try to get into a slow but steady rhythm, and aim to create positive steps angled slightly downwards into the slope and, as with all other steep ground work, resist the temptation to lean in.

When ascending directly, you should aim to create steps which will accommodate at least the front third of your boot – even if you have to kick several times to achieve this. Hold you ice axe in your preferred hand with the pick pointing backwards, and drive the shaft deeply into the snow so that it can be used for support and to assist balance. Only move the axe up once both feet are secure.

When traversing, ascending diagonally or zig-zagging, kick horizontal steps with the side of your boots using a sawing action. Take care when moving up, especially when moving the upslope leg. You are most secure when the leg closest to the slope is in front. Always hold your ice axe in the upslope hand, driving the shaft vertically into the slope above you. When zig-zagging, you should think carefully about where and how you are going to change direction. One method is to kick two good direct steps, change the ice axe to the other hand, then continue. Alternatively you could support yourself with both hands on a well-placed ice axe and turn on your upslope foot. The most simple and straightforward method is to kick a single large step which is big enough to accommodate both feet.

When descending, the best approach is the plunge step. Face away from the slope and use all your body weight to plunge the heel vertically into the snow below you. Keep your toes up and heels down to avoid the chance of rocking forward out of the step and make each move a positive one. Hold your ice axe in your preferred hand and, as in ascent, drive the shaft vertically into the snow to give support.

On steeper slopes where you find the exposure intimidating, face into the slope and kick direct steps as described above. Make sure each step is a positive one before committing your weight to it, and resist the temptation to try and drop too far with each step. Every movement should be comfortable and controlled. If the snow becomes too hard to kick positive steps, you are entering the realm of serious mountaineering and it will be necessary either to cut steps with your axe or to use crampons. Here we come to a problem, for neither step cutting nor crampon technique can be learned safely from a book. They need to be demonstrated practically rather than described theoretically, and then practised in a safe, controlled and preferably supervised environment before being put to use on the hill. Because of this, I do not intend to discuss these techniques in any detail.

With regard to step cutting, even the simple and extremely useful slash step requires a long apprenticeship if it is to be cut safely and effectively in any situation. If you want to learn how to cut steps safely I advise you either to ask an experienced climber to teach you or, better still, to go on a winter skills course run by an MIC or UIAGM qualified instructor.

With regard to crampon technique, it is fair to say that whilst crampons have largely replaced the need to cut steps, they should not be seen as having made step cutting totally redundant. In any case, crampons bring with them their own set of hazards. For example, many types of snow will ball-up under the crampons, compacting into ice and eventually reducing the depth of spike available to pierce the ground and give secure footing. There is obviously a significant difference between walking on metal spikes and blocks of ice.

Additionally, they can slip unexpectedly on verglas or thin ice or when moving over rock steps concealed beneath a thin layer of snow, and unless you adopt a wide-footed gait, the front points have a nasty habit of catching in gaiters and tripping you up. Although the basic foot placement techniques are similar to those mentioned for summer conditions (i.e. feet kept flat to the slope so that all the crampon points bite into the surface), there are several other considerations, especially when changing direction on steep ground. As with step cutting, if you wish to learn how to use crampons safely and effectively, get an experienced climber to show you or enrol on a winter skills course run by an MIC or UIAGM qualified instructor.

Finally, if you are going to venture into the hills in winter conditions you should have a basic understanding of avalanche conditions *(page 211)* and cornices *(page 207)*, and should know something about the effects of cold weather on the body *(section 9)*. Because winter days are so short, it is also advisable to have some idea of winter survival techniques, particularly with regard to emergency shelters *(section 10)*.

## Ice axe arrest

The one ice axe technique which I must mention in a little more detail is that of self arrest, otherwise known as the ice-axe brake. This is a technique which, if used correctly, can prevent a simple slip from becoming something far more serious. It is not an easy technique to master, and needs to be practised at the start of every winter season. You should be able to apply it quickly and effectively from any position; indeed speed and effectiveness are critical factors for the longer you take to apply the brake, the faster you will be travelling, and the more difficult it will be for you to stop. Additionally, although many people practise by sliding feet first on their stomachs, this is the easiest position from which to use the technique and, in practice, you are more likely to be travelling headfirst.

In order to use the technique quickly in the event of a slip, you need to carry and hold your ice axe in the correct way. As soon as you reach the snowline, remove the ice axe from the carrying straps on your rucksack and, unless you intend to use it straight away, slide it diagonally down the back of your rucksack so that it is held in place by a shoulder strap. From this position it can easily be retrieved using one hand.

When carrying the ice axe in your hand, be aware of other people. If you must carry horizontally by the shaft, make sure the pick is pointing down and try not to gouge your companions with the spike. It is far better to hold it by the head with the shaft in a vertical position and the pick pointing backwards. Curve your thumb around and under the back of the adze, and point your index finger down the shaft. Although this may not be as comfortable as some other methods, it is the optimum position from which to apply the self-arrest technique. On sloping ground, always hold your axe in the upslope hand where it can be used to aid balance and give support.

The principle of the ice axe arrest is to use the pick as a friction brake, digging it progressively harder into the snow with your body weight. In order to do this effectively, you need to be in a feet first, face down position with one hand firmly grasping the head of the axe, and with the adze tucked firmly into the hollow just below your collarbone. The shaft should be brought across your chest so that the other hand can hold the end of the shaft and cover the spike to prevent it sticking into either the snow or you. Your legs should be kept apart to give some stability, with your feet lifted well clear of the snow (figure 14). Keeping the feet up is especially impor-

*Figure 14: Basic self arrest position (viewed from the underside)*

tant if you are wearing crampons for otherwise the front points can catch and flip you into a backward somersault. Having said this, the feet can be used as an aid to braking just before you come to rest.

The best way to apply the brake is to pull down on the head of the ice axe, at the same time pulling the spike away from the slope. This will have the effect of rolling you over the adze so that the maximum amount of body weight can be applied. Tucking your elbows into your sides and arching your back will enhance the effect still further. Do not lift your head as this will lift your shoulders – indeed, the brim of your helmet (recommended when practising even if you decide not to wear one when winter walking) should be so close to the slope that there should be snow inside your helmet when you stop!

It is vitally important that weight is applied to the pick gradually or else it will catch suddenly and could be ripped out of your grasp. If you are a little too enthusiastic and the adze is pulled from its correct position in the hollow below your collarbone you may have difficulty in relocating it simply by pulling up on it. If this happens, lift your head so as to release the weight, relocate the adze in the correct position and then, and only then, try again.

What I have described so far is the basic position for the ice axe arrest – the simplest of all the scenarios. You may have to remember all this whilst plummeting down an icy slope with increasing velocity towards an awesome drop (or simply a pile of boulders)! In all probability you will be scared out of your wits. You will, no doubt, therefore appreciate that this most basic of winter skills requires practice, more practice, and yet more practice. In all probability you will not be sliding feet first on your front, but head first, possibly on your back, or even rolling or somersaulting, so what I have described becomes the final stage in a sequence of manoeuvres.

No matter which way you are falling, you must get yourself into this basic position and grip the ice axe correctly (one hand over the head with the pick away from you and the adze located under your collarbone, shaft across your body, and the other hand holding the base of the shaft and covering the spike). If you are rolling or somersaulting you must also try to stabilise yourself by spreading your arms and legs as wide as possible – not easy and possibly very painful.

If you are sliding head first, face down, gently push the pick into the snow as far to one side of you as possible so you swing round into a feet first position. If you are sliding on your back, get onto your front by rolling towards the hand holding the head of the ice axe. Never roll towards the hand holding the spike or else the pick will bite suddenly and the axe could be torn from your grasp. If you are falling headfirst on your back you have serious problems. The best manoeuvre involves holding the ice axe across your body and pushing the pick into the snow by your side. As you begin to spin around, roll your body around the shaft to end up in the right position. This sounds complicated – it *is* complicated. When practising these manoeuvres, do so from all positions and with the axe held in both hands. Always wear a helmet and use a high concave slope with a good, obstacle-free run-out at the bottom.

# River crossings

The last skill I wish to mention is that of crossing rivers. I would hazard a guess that most people seriously underestimate the force of even shallow moving water and, whilst fording rivers is not a common cause of mountain fatalities, people do drown every year. The best advice on fording a swollen river is don't; the best method of crossing a river is via a bridge! If crossing is imperative and there is no bridge, consult your map in case there is an area within striking distance where the stream splits into several channels. If not, head upstream looking for a suitable crossing point. Sites to avoid are those near bends or rapids, and the water at a wide crossing is generally shallower and slower (and thus safer) than at a narrow crossing. Wherever you cross, beware of underwater hazards such as submerged rocks, and flood debris. Walk along the bank in both up- and downstream directions so that you can view the crossing point from as many angles as possible. If you can also get a high vantage point, so much the better.

Before attempting a crossing, remove your socks and either roll up your trouser legs or remove them completely. Not only will this prevent you from having to continue with saturated clothing, but it will also reduce the potential drag as any material will increase the resistance and therefore make you more likely to be swept off your feet. You should, however, wear your boots. You should also close your rucksack tightly so as to trap air inside it. Although the buoyancy in a rucksack can be a life-saver in an emergency, it can also cause grave problems, for if it is strapped to your back and you slip, it will tend to force you face down in the water. You should therefore undo any waist or chest straps and loosen the shoulder straps so you can remove it quickly if necessary.

When crossing, keep your feet well apart and take short, shuffling steps, always ensuring that one foot is firmly placed before moving the other. Do not cross your legs as this could throw you off balance. Face upstream so you get warning of any flood debris coming towards you and so there is no danger of the current buckling your knees. The safest crossing techniques involve teamwork, either using the linked-arms method or the huddle method *(figure 15)*. Solo crossing is not recommended, but if it is necessary try to present a diagonal profile to the river and, if possible, support yourself on the upstream side with whatever is available – walking stick, ice axe, tent pole, etc. *(figure 16)*. The use of ropes is not recommended because if you are taken downstream when held on a rope, the force of water will drag you

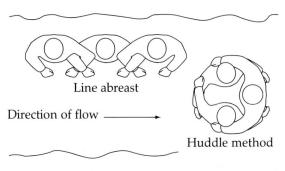

Line abreast

Direction of flow ⟶

Huddle method

*Figure 15: Group river crossing*

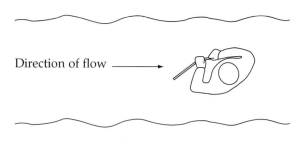

*Figure 16: Solo river crossing method*

under. If you are unlucky enough to be swept off your feet, try to hold your rucksack across your chest and manoeuvre yourself into a position whereby you are heading downstream feet first. This will not be easy, but it is extremely important as the most common causes of drowning in this situation are hitting boulders headfirst and getting trapped by a heel hook. This is where a person floating headfirst downstream on their back gets an ankle trapped between two rocks. If this happens the pressure of water flowing against the body pushes it under and makes it virtually impossible to escape. Do not fight the current (it will always win!). Go with it taking the occasional stroke in an attempt to reach slower or shallower water near a bank or along the inside of any bend.

# 4    Camping equipment

There is something primitive and totally captivating about camping beside a clear mountain tarn amid gaunt crags, miles away from civilisation. If the weather is pleasant it can be a source of endless delight, but if the weather is malevolent it can turn into an unmitigated disaster with potentially serious consequences. Having said this, with the right equipment and skills, even bad-weather camping can be comfortable and satisfying.

In this section we are going to look at a range of basic camping equipment. As elsewhere in this book I have deliberately steered away from mentioning specific models, concentrating instead on basic design considerations. The outdoor market is so big nowadays that new models and innovations come and go with a speed which is nothing short of confusing. I work on the basis that as long as you know what you want from your equipment and what it needs to do then you should be able to visit your local friendly gear shop and make an educated choice when confronted with four or five things which all purport to do the same thing better than each other. Forget about the marketing hype and look at the basic design and quality of the materials and workmanship.

Space precludes the inclusion of detailed information. If you want to do any serious wild camping, you should know a little more about the equipment than I am able to give here. Suitable reference sources are to be found in the list of further reading at the back of this book.

## Tents

Personal preference and budgetary considerations aside, a tent suitable for use in the mountains needs to fulfil a number of functions. It should, for example, be light in weight and low in bulk, weatherproof and stable, and simple to pitch, strike and pack. Unfortunately, in practice many of these are mutually exclusive, so in essence there is no such thing as the ideal mountain tent.

Since the advent of flexible tent poles, there has been something of a revolution in tent design. In addition to the standard ridge tent, there are now several variations on the theme plus wedge tents, tunnel tents, single hoop tents, crossover dome

*Figure 17: generalised comparison of tent designs*

| Type | Stability | Space-weight ratio | Cooking storage |
|------|-----------|--------------------|-----------------|
| Standard ridge | excellent | poor | fair |
| Sloping ridge | fair | fair | poor |
| Transverse ridge | fair | good | good |
| Wedge | poor | fair | fair |
| Single hoop | good | good | poor |
| Tunnel | poor | fair | poor |
| Crossover dome | good | good | good |
| Geodesic dome | good | good | good |

tents, and geodesic dome tents. Luckily, there is a simple way through this maze of shape as, in essence, there are still only three basic designs: ridge tents, tunnel tents, and dome tents. There are also a few hybrid designs in which manufacturers have tried to make use of the best features of each basic shape. The main features, advantages and disadvantages of each are illustrated in *figure 17*.

The main function of a mountain tent is to give shelter from the elements. To do this effectively it should be of a double skin construction. This means there should be an inner compartment which is totally enclosed by an outer layer (the flysheet) which reaches to the ground on all sides thus protecting both the walls and doors of the inner tent. The inner tent should have a sewn-in ground-sheet made from a durable and totally waterproof material, and this should extend up the walls for at least 10cms and form a lip at the doors. The gap between the inner compartment and the flysheet is extremely important. Not only does it provide a degree of insulation but, more important, it plays an essential role in weatherproofing.

It goes without saying that the quality of both materials and workmanship should be of the highest standard. All seams should be lap-felled (where the two layers of fabric are brought together then wrapped around each other before being sewn), and secured by a lock stitch rather than a chain stitch which can run if a fault develops. The quality of the stitching is crucial, especially at stress areas such as pegging points, pole sleeves, apexes, ends of zips, and seam junctions. Major stress areas should be reinforced in some way such as by bar tacking.

The flysheet should preferably be made from a totally waterproof fabric, although this is not absolutely essential, and should be big enough to give sufficient space in which to store gear and, ideally, to cook during inclement weather. In theory, if water does penetrate the flysheet fabric it will run down the inside surface and will therefore not reach the inner compartment. This is fine so long as the separation between the inner and outer layers is maintained.

If the two layers touch then inevitably water will penetrate the inner. Although at first glance it appears that the simplest way around this problem is to use a totally waterproof material for both the inner compartment and flysheet, in practice this causes more problems than it solves. In the same way that condensation can be a problem with totally waterproof shell garments, it can also be a problem in totally waterproof tents. What is needed, therefore, is an inner compartment made from a permeable fabric which will allow water vapour to pass through and condense on the inside surface of the flysheet. Here again, maintaining the separation between the inner and outer layers is critical. This important gap between the two layers is easier to maintain in some designs than in others.

Even in the best designed tents, condensation can occur within the inner tent in certain weather conditions, especially if you are forced to cook inside the tent. Mesh panels can help to alleviate this problem as can two way zips which allow you to open the door from the top to create ventilation.

The way in which the tent is pitched will obviously vary from model to model. There are certain things worth bearing in mind. For example, if you find it difficult to pitch the tent on a calm day in a perfect valley site, think what it will be like trying to do the same thing in a howling gale at a less than perfect high camp. To a degree, the simpler the design, the better, and ease of pitching and striking is an important factor. Moreover, during camping trips of two or more nights, it is a distinct advantage to have a tent which pitches outer first. If the weather is inclement, a tent of this design will allow you to do the vast majority of your packing and unpacking under cover of the flysheet.

The only single-skin tents suitable for use in the mountains are those made of a breathable water-proof material such as Goretex. Although these are obviously light and compact, in practice these do not work too well in temperate climates unless you are very large and they are very small. This is simply because it is difficult to maintain a climate inside the tent which is warmer and more moist than the climate outside the tent. Having said this, it would be remiss of me not to mention bivi-bags.

These breathable-fabric sacks work extremely well and, whilst less comfortable and convenient than a tent, may be of interest to those who enjoy a Spartan existence. Some are available with flexible hoops which make them similar to a very small tunnel tent. There is, of course, no room to store gear, and no space in which to cook in inclement weather. You simply put your sleeping bag inside the bivi-bag, get in, and zip everything up!

The poles and pegs supplied with your tent can vary greaty in quality. Generally, hollow alloy poles are better than glassfibre poles although both have disadvantages. Alloy poles are prone to kinking whilst the cheaper glassfibre poles can shatter and get split ends. Poles of composite materials (including carbon fibre) are also available and these are generally very good.

Few tent manufacturers supply a good selection of pegs. Many seem to supply only a handful of steel skewers. Some pegs stick better in different terrain than others, so it is worth taking a selection of pegs including alloy skewers as general purpose pegs, plus a handful of angles, maybe one or two screw-in types, and a couple of storm anchors. A good retailer will be able to show you a wide range and explain the pros and cons of each type.

Finally, a good mountain tent is not going to be cheap, so it pays to see a range of models before you choose. When making the choice, ask yourself a number of questions such as how much room will you need, will you be using the tent for brief, overnight stops or as a base for longer stays, at what time of year will it be used, etc. Beware of models labelled "mountain tent" – although there are some excellent tents labelled thus they are often designed for use at high altitude in dry, cold conditions and are therefore totally unsuitable for our wet and windy mountains.

## Sleeping bags

As with your tent, your sleeping bag should be light, compact and of good quality. Its main purpose is to keep you warm by preventing heat loss, the efficiency with which it can do this being quoted in terms of a season rating, this going from two season to five season! A two season bag is suitable for valley use in summer conditions; a three season bag for use in all but winter conditions except in valley sites; a four season bag for year round use except in extreme conditions such as those often encountered during high level camps in winter; a five season bag for high level camps in all conditions.

Both the construction of the sleeping bag and the type and quality of the insulation have a bearing on the season rating. There are two main types of insulation, these being natural materials and synthetic materials.

Most of the synthetic fillings suitable for use in the mountains will be based on some form of hollow polyester fibres, the best of these being only slightly inferior to the better natural fillings. In some sleeping bags, these fibres will have been formed into layers (known as batts) held together with resin. In others the fibres remain loose in which case the sleeping bag will be described as being blown filled. The use of terylene fibres in sleeping bags which are to be used in the mountains is not recommended as it is too heavy and bulky. There are two main advantages to be gained by using synthetic fillings. Firstly, unlike natural fillings, they retain much of their insulation qualities when wet. Secondly, they are cheaper! On the negative side, sleeping bags with synthetic fillings are generally heavier and more bulky than similarly rated bags with natural fillings, even though this difference may be minimal in the more expensive models. Additionally, they do not transmit water vapour as well as natural fillings (particularly those using batts), and this tends to make them feel sticky.

Natural fillings suitable for use in the mountains include down and down-feather mixes. Kapok is totally unsuitable. Pure eiderdown is extremely rare; most modern bags use either goose down, duck down, or down and down/feather mixes. The biggest advantages of using natural fillings is that they result in a sleeping bag which is lighter and more compact than a similarly rated bag filled with a synthetic material. They also have a warm, luxurious feel which tends to be lacking in bags using synthetic fillings. Apart from the price, the biggest disadvantage is that they lose most if not all of their insulation qualities if they get wet. For this reason it is imperative that these sleeping bags are kept dry. Using waterproof fabrics in the construction of the bag is not the answer due to the problems of condensation (see pages 27 and 114), and although bags using breathable waterproof fabrics are available, you will probably need a friendly bank manager if you wish to buy one.

Perhaps the simplest way to put the differences between synthetic and natural fillings into perspective is to say that, warmth for warmth, the best quality synthetic filled bags are slightly heavier, fractionally more bulky, but less expensive than their natural-filled counterparts.

The construction of the sleeping bag is also of the utmost importance, particularly with natural fillings and blown filled synthetics. A sleeping bag is basically two sacks of material with insulation between them, and if the gap between the outer and inner sacks is not compartmentalised in some way, the filling moves about causing cold spots. Although simple quilting will stop this movement, there will be cold spots along all the seams. What is needed, therefore, is some form of baffle between the inner and outer sack, the most common designs being shown in *figure 18*. Heat loss can also occur from the foot of the bag, and the baffling should continue in this area in the form of a box-foot.

The shape of the bag is really a matter of personal preference, although some form of hood can be of great benefit on cold nights. The most important consideration is that of comfort. Whatever the shape, there should be either some form of shoulder baffle or some method by which the bag can be tightened above the shoulders to prevent heat loss. Zips are, again, very much a matter of personal preference although they can make a high season rating bag more adaptable as they can be used for ventilation during warmer weather. If you choose a sleeping bag with zips, make sure they are well baffled.

The material from which the inner and outer sacks are made has a vital role. With natural and blown-

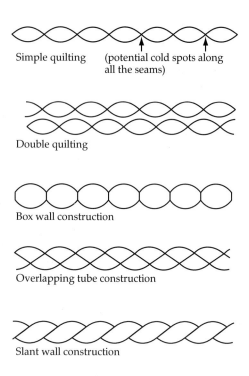

Simple quilting    (potential cold spots along all the seams)

Double quilting

Box wall construction

Overlapping tube construction

Slant wall construction

*Figure 18: Baffle designs in sleeping bags*

filled synthetic materials in particular, it should be of a tight weave (down-proof) so that it does not allow any of the filling to escape. It should also be durable, rot-proof, light in weight and low in bulk. Additionally, because the human body loses a considerable amount of water during sleep, it needs to be permeable. Nylon fabrics are commonly used, although many people prefer a sleeping bag with a slightly heavier and bulkier polycotton inner as this tends to be more comfortable.

Choosing a sleeping bag suitable for all seasons can be difficult – those bags suitable for early autumn are not good enough for winter use, whilst those suitable for winter use are too hot for late spring. One answer lies in the use of sleeping bag liners made from polypropylene (i.e. thermal underwear fabric) or fibre-pile. These often have a season rating of one, and can therefore transform a three season bag into a four season bag, and so on. These liners are useful in their own right as items of emergency equipment. Being reasonably light in weight and low in bulk they can easily be carried in your rucksack during spring and autumn where they may be extremely useful in the event of benightment or an emergency. However, they should not be seen as a substitute for a conventional sleeping bag during serious trips in winter conditions.

## Sleepmats

Like the thermal layers of clothing, the insulation in sleeping bags works by trapping air. When you lie down, you compress the filling reducing the amount of air which can be trapped and thus reducing the efficiency of the insulation. No matter how good your sleeping bag, you will therefore need a sleepmat to insulate you from the cold ground.

A standard sleepmat consists of a rectangle of closed cell foam which is placed between the sleeping bag and the groundsheet providing a cushioning effect in addition to extra insulation. Although these are widely available, their price varies considerably so it is worth shopping around. Make sure the foam is closed cell not open cell – the latter works like a sponge and will absorb and trap water. Sleepmats are available in a range of different thickness and are sometimes given a season rating similar to sleeping bags. Also available are inflatable sleepmats which, although heavier and slightly more bulky (and a lot more expensive), give far more comfort and insulation.

Finally, if your tent has a thin groundsheet, or if you camp on a regular basis, you might like to consider buying a groundsheet liner. This is basically like thin (3mm) sleepmat, again of closed cell foam, and is usually sold off the roll. Unlike sleepmats, however, it is placed beneath the groundsheet where it gives protection in addition to extra cushioning and insulation. In all but the warmest conditions, however, it should not be used as a substitute for a sleepmat but as an enhancement.

## Stoves

An efficient lightweight stove is an essential item of kit when you are camping maybe several long and difficult miles from the nearest habitation. As with most other types of modern equipment, at first glance there is a bewildering range of stoves available using a variety of different fuels. However, all these can be divided into three broad categories, these being gas stoves, methylated spirits stoves and pressure stoves. It is also possible to buy light and compact stoves using solid fuel tablets or a form of jelly fuel. Whilst these may have a use as items of emergency equipment *(see section 10)*, they are unsuitable for use as the main source of cooking heat when camping and should not be regarded as alternatives to the types of stove described below.

Gas stoves are available in an ever-growing range of shapes and sizes including models which come complete with their own pan in which they can be stored when being carried. There are two main types: those using resealable cartridges, and those using non-resealable cartridges. Those using resealable cartridges are arguably more convenient as they can be dismantled and carried more easily in the rucksack. Many of these stoves are highly efficient and, of course, they are very convenient. All you have to do is turn on the gas and light them (some will even do this for you!), so they are superb for making a quick brew in the early hours of the morning.

However, they do have several disadvantages. Even if you disregard the fact that they are very expensive to run, the cylinders may not be widely available in remote areas, and you will soon find out that they tend to burn with an infuriatingly low flame once the cylinder is less than about half full. A half full cylinder, of course, takes up the same amount of space as a full one, and if you are away for some time, you may have to carry quite a few (as well as bringing the empties back). Even if you use a burner shield and a new cylinder, they hate draughts and tend to blow out at the slightest provocation. This is particularly apparent in cold conditions.

Indeed, butane (the most common gas) is impossible

to light in temperatures of below about freezing, and although it is possible to buy cylinders filled with propane which will burn at lower temperatures, it is fair to say that gas stoves and cold weather do not mix. One way around this problem is to sleep with your stove or its cylinders. Whilst this does work you should be aware of the danger of leaking gas. Not only could this suffocate you, but because the gas is heavier than air it can lie in a layer trapped within the tray of the sewn-in groundsheet just waiting for you to strike a match to make a morning brew.

Modern methylated spirits stoves bear little resemblance to the old fashioned picnic stoves. Indeed, the better models are cheap to run and surprisingly efficient, are quick and easy to light and give full heat within seconds. The most common models come as units complete with nesting pans (and even a kettle if you want one) which means that they represent excellent value for money, particularly for first time buyers. They are also the only type of stoves available which thrive on draughts. On the negative side, although the fuel is reasonably easy to get it is heavy and fast-burning, so not only do you have to refill the stove at regular intervals, you also have to carry a fair amount of fuel with you.

Additionally, the flame control on most models is fairly basic to say the least, the adjustments being full heat, simmer or off. Methylated spirits will seek out any weakness in the container in which it is carried, so use a proper fuel bottle with a well-threaded, deep neck *(see below)* and make sure the seal is in good condition. Although any spilled fuel will evaporate fairly quickly, refuelling should be done with the utmost care as the fuel burns with an almost invisible flame and accidents have occurred when people have tried to refill stoves which were still lit. To minimise the danger of this, refill your stove each time you come to use it and, whenever possible, allow it to cool down before attempting to refill it. Finally, meths will make the bottom of your pans sooty. Although this can be avoided by adding a small amount of water to the fuel, a blackened pot will absorb heat better than a shiny silver one so is therefore more efficient.

Pressure stoves come in a wide variety of models and types, some burning paraffin, some burning petrol, and some purporting to burn anything from sump oil to vodka. Generally speaking they are extremely efficient, very economical, and most have a stupendous heat output. The purr of a pressure stove is a comforting sound, especially if you are trapped in your tent during a storm! The fuel, either petrol or paraffin, is usually simple to obtain even in remote areas, but you must remember that these fuels are not interchangeable – a paraffin stove filled with petrol will behave like an incendiary bomb!

On the negative side, most of these stoves are heavy, bulky and expensive to buy. There are exceptions to this, the most obvious being those stoves which come simply as a burner and tube with a pump of the end. These are designed to be used in conjunction with a fuel bottle, the pump being used to pressurise it. It must be noted, too, that pressure stoves are not the most convenient of stoves, for all but a very few require priming or pre-heating. Not only can this be frustrating if all you want is a quick brew, but it is also potentially extremely dangerous for if not done correctly it can result in a flare – in which a fountain of burning liquid sprays out of the burner.

Of the two major fuels, paraffin is the cheaper and the least affected by ambient temperature. Indeed, paraffin pressure stoves usually include a pump so they can be pressurised by hand, and these stoves will work well whilst sitting directly on snow. However, although the vapour is not flammable, if you spill paraffin it takes ages to evaporate and makes everything near it stink for weeks afterwards. Additionally, you will need to carry either meths or solid fuel tablets in order to prime the stove correctly.

Petrol, on the other hand, will evaporate quickly, but please note that any spillage can be extremely dangerous because the vapour is explosively flammable. Only use unleaded fuel (or the more expensive camp-stove fuel) or else the jet of the burner will become blocked with monotonous regularity. Additionally, the petrol can, with care, be used to prime the stove, although many manu-facturers recommend the use of a priming paste instead. Paste is certainly safer. On the down side, many petrol stoves are self-pressurising and can be difficult to light in cold conditions. Admittedly, some models have optional pumps which replace the filler cap, but even when these are used you need to insulate the stove from the ground in some way.

Although multi-fuel stoves would seem to solve many of the problems associated with fuel availability in remote areas, they vary widely in performance. Although there are some very efficient models, others are quite complex and require setting up before each use. If choosing one of these stoves you would be wise to play with it in the shop and to read the instructions before parting with any cash.

If using anything other than a gas stove, you will need something in which to carry the liquid fuel. This should be specifically designed for carrying fuel (not an old water flask). The most common fuel bottles are made of aluminium and have well-threaded, deep necks and plastic stoppers with replaceable sealing washers. The efficiency of the seal is very important, especially if carrying methylated spirits which will seek out any weakness and exploit it. Never use your fuel bottle for water nor your water flask for fuel; this could lead to obvious contamination and confusion.

Particularly with pressure stoves, it is important that you get to know how they work before you use them in the wild. If you have never used a pressure stove before, I advise you to light it in your back garden first, just in case you get a flare. Once you are happy with the lighting technique, try cooking yourself a meal on it in the comfort of your own kitchen, and then imagine what it would be like doing the same in the cramped confines of your tent during stormy weather.

Finally, it is of little use taking a stove if you have nothing with which to light it. Even if your stove is described as having automatic ignition you would be wise to carry something to use in the event that the technology fails. Non-safety matches are useful, especially if you dip them in varnish to make them waterproof, and a cigarette lighter can be worth its weight in gold, especially if it is a petrol lighter and you have a petrol stove. If you carry a lighter, you must keep it dry or the flint will refuse to spark. Lifeboat matches (which are both waterproof and windproof) are a useful standby for those really wet and windy nights.

## Pans and utensils

If you have a methylated spirits stove, there will be no need for you to buy any pans as they are usually an integral part of the stove. However, with pressure and most gas stoves, you will need something in which to cook your food. In general terms you have a choice between mess tins, nesting billy cans (or dixies), and cooksets.

Of the three types, cooksets are the most convenient, the better ones containing a couple of deep pans with lids, a frying pan and, perhaps, a bowl and a universal handle. Although aluminium is the usual material, slightly heavier but more durable stainless steel cooksets are available in which one or more of the pans have copper bases. These transmit the heat far more evenly and are therefore more efficient.

When it comes to eating your food, do you really need crockery? Why not eat straight from the pan? Alternatively, take a deep, bendy plastic plate which will double as a bowl. Plastic cutlery has the nasty habit of breaking at the most inappropriate of times, standard kitchen cutlery tends to be heavy, so the best option is a cutlery clip-set designed for camping. These are usually made from lightweight alloy and are reasonably cheap and durable.

If you are carrying a vacuum flask you can use the attached cup for your drinks. If not, or if you want something with more capacity, a bendy plastic mug is the best. Avoid metal mugs – it is virtually impossible to drink the contents whilst they are hot because the hot metal burns your lips.

## Lighting

If you intend to camp, some form of lighting is essential. In its simplest form this will be a candle, stubby long-life candles being the most convenient. These give out a surprising amount of light and heat, especially if used in conjunction with a reflector made of silver foil. If using candles inside the tent, take great care and make sure they are kept well away from the fabric. Placing them on an upturned pan is a good ploy as they will usually go out if accidentally knocked over. Alternatively, there are some excellent lightweight candle lanterns available which fold down when not in use. One useful aspect of candles is that they give off heat as well as light.

A torch is obviously useful, but make sure it is robust and waterproof. Most convenient is a headtorch, those with the battery container as an integral part of the headband being the most practical. Remember to keep batteries separate from the torch when not in use, and take spare batteries (and possibly bulbs) with you.

Although it is possible to buy excellent gas and pressure lanterns, these are generally too heavy and bulky to be of much use during short trips to the wilds. However, they can be worth their weight in gold during extended trips at base camps.

## Rucksacks

All of the features needed in a good daysack *(see section 2)* should also be present in a good backpacking rucksack. It should, for example, be simple in design and construction, and shaped in such a way that the load is carried high on your back. However, because you will need extra space and will be carrying a lot more weight, there are certain additional requirements.

A modern backpacking rucksack is a scientifically designed piece of equipment which should be chosen with as much care as your boots. Depending on the type of camping you intend to do, it should have a capacity of between 55 and 75 litres. Unless you are off on a mammoth expedition, if you feel you need a rucksack larger than this it is probably worth checking whether your packing technique could be improved or whether all the items you are carrying are essential.

Many backpacking rucksacks are split horizontally into two compartments, the upper one being access-ible through the top flap, the lower one via a zipped opening about two thirds of the way down the body of the sack. This zip should preferably be two-way and well baffled. The two compartments are often separated by a baffle. It is useful if this is zipped (and therefore removable) or only attached at the front and the back so that long items (such as tent poles) can be slid down the length of the rucksack on either side. In addition, many models are available with side pockets (some of which are removable), and these can be useful for carrying things needed en route or keeping items such as liquid fuels well away from other objects which they could contaminate.

The most important difference between a daysack and a backpacking rucksack is the way in which the load is carried. In a daysack it is the shoulder straps which do most of the work; in a good backpacking rucksack, however, there should be some form of load-bearing hip belt which enables most of the weight to be transferred directly onto the pelvic girdle. In order for it to do this efficiently, your rucksack should fit you correctly. Not only should the back of the rucksack mirror the curvature of your spine, but also the hip belt should be in the correct position, fitting snugly across the top of your hips, not around your waist.

Although some harness systems are adjustable, many rucksacks come in a variety of lengths and you should make sure you get one which fits you correctly. The main purpose of the shoulder straps is to prevent the rucksack from slipping backwards. Because they are worn fairly loose there are times when they can slip off your shoulders, so some rucksacks come with a short chest-strap which holds the shoulder straps in the correct position.

The body-hugging fit of the rucksack means that

there can be problems with a build-up of condensation across your back. Some manufacturers have gone to great lengths to try and solve this problem, with chevron shaped panels and air vents. These are often less than successful, and if you go camping in warm weather on a regular basis, a damp back is something you will soon get used to.

## Useful items

The equipment described so far represents the essentials – with it and your standard hill walking kit, you can exist in the mountains in relative comfort. However, most experienced campers take a few extra bits and pieces. These include food containers (made of plastic – never of glass), water purification tablets (sterilising water by boiling takes at least 20 minutes and uses precious fuel), collapsible water carriers, paracord, toilet paper, sharp knife preferably with a tin opener, soap-filled scouring pad, small sponge, jeycloth, toothbrush & comb, silver foil, plastic bags, inflatable pillow, basic tent repair kit, etc.

Only you can decide what extra items you need; only you can justify the extra weight or the space they take up. Most people take far too much on their first few trips. Make a list of what you take and cross off anything you do not use. Do not take these the next time you go unless, of course, they would be useful or essential in an emergency.

# 5    Camping skills

Although many people think of camping as roughing it, the experience need not be an uncomfortable one. However, even if you have the very best equipment, you will still need certain skills if you are to get the most out of your stay. It is not the possession of the equipment that keeps you safe and comfortable so much as the knowledge of what to do with it and how to use it best.

## Sites

Assuming you have the basic minimum of good quality equipment as outlined in the last section, the most important consideration is choice of site. Choose this with care. Try to find somewhere which is reasonably level, and place the groundsheet on a flat area where there are no lumps such as tussocks or protruding rocks which will make sleeping uncomfortable. The site should be well drained, but should be within easy walking distance of a water supply. Sites near streams and lakes can be idyllic, but they may also be cold, noisy, and damp, and at certain times of year you will be plagued by insects. Bear in mind, too, that mountain streams can rise very quickly during rain; your welcoming brookside site will not seem so pleasant if it becomes covered with water in the early hours.

The most important factor of all is that of shelter,

particularly from the wind. Because weather conditions can change with frightening speed in the mountains, always choose your site with the worst in mind, and pitch your tent with its back facing the direction of the prevailing wind. It is far easier to secure your camp from the outset than it is to try and adjust everything in the pitch black in the middle of an unexpected storm. Think about the type of shelter you want – pitching your tent in the shelter of a large cliff may not seem like such a good idea if a rock lands on you in the early hours. Similarly, pitching beneath trees can be a frightening experience during a storm.

Camping in winter is a whole different ball game, and you should have a reasonable amount of summer camping experience before deciding to camp in the mountains in winter conditions. Choosing a sheltered site is critical, but beware the problems of drifting snow which always builds up on the leeside. If there is snow, stamp out an area slightly larger than the tent before pitching, and bank consolidated snow against the base of the flysheet to help prevent spindrift collecting in the gap between flysheet and inner tent. Snow is very heavy, and can easily collapse a tent if allowed to build up on the flysheet. Some tents are more prone than others.

## Cooking

The vast majority of camping injuries are burns and scalds. Take extra care when you are cooking and try to work methodically. Lay everything out beforehand so that everything you want is close to hand. If you are going to be at the site for any length of time, it is a good idea to prepare a cooking area where you can place your stove on a solid, flat surface. Cook outside whenever possible, and always hold the pan when adjusting the flame or stirring the contents. If you are forced to cook inside the tent because of awful weather, appoint one person to do the cooking, place the stove on a solid, non-flammable base near the doorway and keep everyone else well away, either in the back of the tent or, if there are a few of you, in another tent.

Avoid putting hot pans directly on the groundsheet unless you want neat round holes! If your tent has space for you to cook beneath the flysheet, so much the better. Wherever you cook, keep the stove well away from any fabric or flammable material, and take extra care when refuelling. Always use lids as these save heat (and therefore fuel), and always boil slightly more water than you think you will need.

The quality of the food you produce can make or break a camping trip for you will undoubtedly have a ravenous appetite. Try to choose food which is nutritious and easy to prepare as well as being compact and light. If necessary, remove food from its original packaging and repack it to make it easier to carry, and remember that there is usually a fair amount of useful space inside pans. Dehydrated foods are a good choice; freeze dried foods are even better as they require far less cooking time.

Some things such as quick cook rice and pasta can be brought to the boil and then left to cook in their own heat whilst you prepare something else. Stews of any description are good, especially if you take a little curry powder with you. Whatever you take, make sure it is something you like – it is pointless taking something which is convenient if you do not feel like eating it. In particular, you should have plenty of high energy foods with you, and no matter how tired you are nor how awful the weather, always try to have a hot meal each night and a substantial breakfast each morning. The food you carry is particularly important on extended trips when you plan to be away from civilisation for several days. In this situation you would be wise to plan your menus and to read something about expedition rationing and nutrition.

## Load packing and carrying

No matter how fit you are nor how good your rucksack, the way you pack your load will have a considerable bearing on both the psychological weight (i.e. the weight you feel) and comfort. The most important considerations are to make the best use of all space, and to pack the rucksack in such a way that the load is balanced and bears directly onto the pelvic girdle and thus onto the legs.

Additionally, you should give some thought to the order in which you are going to need the various items you are carrying – it is not much use burying stuff you need en route beneath items you will not need until you have pitched camp. Try to avoid packing sharp or hard objects where they will dig into your back, and resist the temptation to strap lots of items to the outside of the rucksack where they will swing around or catch on things. Although everyone has their own way of packing a

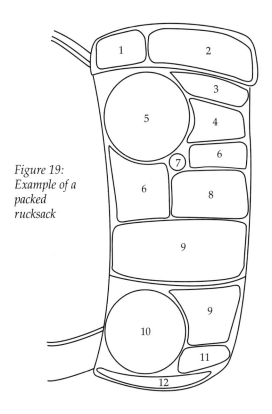

Figure 19:
Example of a
packed
rucksack

| | | |
|---|---|---|
| 1 First aid | 7 Torch | 12 Survival bag |
| 2 Items needed during the day | 8 Cooking pans etc | Note: heavier items towards the top |
| 3 Waterproofs | 9 Clothing etc | |
| 4 Stove | 10 Sleeping bag | |
| 5 Tent | 11 Emergency rations | |
| 6 Food | | |

rucksack, it is not insignificant that many experienced mountaineers pack in a remarkably similar way.

The sleeping bag, possibly contained within a compression sack, goes at the bottom of the rucksack together with spare clothing; the tent, stove and possibly some food goes towards the top, and items needed en route are either packed in side pockets, the top pouch pocket, or at the very top. No matter how good the container, liquid fuels are best packed in side pockets well away from any foodstuffs. Sleepmats can either be rolled tightly and strapped to the top or bottom of the rucksack, or can be opened out as used as a liner inside. A typical example of a packed rucksack is shown in *figure 19*.

## Camp hygiene

A mild stomach upset which may cause only minor irritation when at home can be a serious problem when camping at a remote site several strenuous miles from habitation, so it pays to think about camp hygiene. Most of the hygiene factors are obvious. When camping at a lakeside site, for example, collect water from the inflow and do your washing and toilet near the outflow. Make sure your hands are clean before preparing or eating food, and wash the pans after you have finished. It is far easier to do this immediately than to wake up the following morning to find you have to get rid of congealed grease and burn-on food before you can have breakfast.

Although it is not strictly necessary to dig a latrine if you are only using a site for one night, any faeces should be buried at least 15cms deep and used toilet paper should be burnt, the ash being buried with the faeces. If there is a group of you, or if you are staying at the same site for more than a day or so, you should dig a simple latrine. This does not have to be anything spectacular – a simple trench not less that 30cms deep will suffice. Remove the turves and stack them to one side so they can be replaced when you leave. If you feel it is necessary to dig a latrine, you may also need to dig a grease pit in which to pour all your dirty water. This only need be a simple hole in the ground but remember to remove and save the turves and to replace them afterwards. Within 24hrs of you leaving a wild site it should be impossible to tell that anyone had camped there.

Personal hygiene is also fairly important. Any cuts and abrasions should be treated as soon as possible by washing and then using an antiseptic cream, and particular attention should be paid to the feet, especially on longer trips.

## Camp routine

Although the very term routine may be anathema to some people who go off into the wilds to get away from that sort of thing, there can be little doubt that having some form of routine or sequence of events can go a long way towards making the camping experience less prone to discomfort or disaster. This is particularly true during wet weather, when move-ment in and out of the tent should be kept to the absolute minimum. Although different people will have slightly different routines, the following should give some idea of the type of things you should have regard for.

Unless you know the site well, try to arrive early so that you have plenty of time in which to set up camp. Assuming that the weather is not so bad that you need to get under shelter immediately, a brew on arrival is a great morale booster. While the water is heating, try to get the feel of the site and work out the best position for the tent(s). Pitching should be done carefully and methodically having first cleared an area slightly larger than the ground-sheet of any sharp stones.

Different tents are erected in different ways, and most are difficult to pitch in windy weather, particularly if you have never done it before. Make sure, therefore, that you are familiar with your tent before you use it in the mountains so that you can pitch it neatly and reasonably quickly. Ensure that pegs are placed firmly at an angle of between 60° and 45° to the angle of strain, and if you use boulders to weigh down dubious pegs, make sure the rock cannot chafe the guyline. No matter how tired you are nor how bad the weather, it is far easier to make minor adjustments at this stage than in the teeth of a storm at three o'clock the following morning.

Once you are satisfied with the tent, lay out your sleepmat and sleeping bag, and position all other items so they are readily accessible when needed. If it is raining, think carefully about what you are doing so as to keep movement in and out of the tent to a minimum, remove your wet gear before entering the tent and if any water does find its way into the inner tent, mop it up immediately before it has a chance to spread. In winter conditions, it is very easy to lose things when it is snowing, so put everything in a definite place and do not leave anything lying around.

Do not allow snow to build up on the flysheet. Either clear it off from the outside or, if ensconced inside, bang the inner against the fly at regular intervals in an attempt to dislodge it. No matter what the weather, never wear boots inside the tent.

As has already been noted, a hot evening meal is essential, and you should make every effort to cook one no matter what. Before turning in, lay out everything ready for breakfast the next morning, and if it is cold, have a final brew and make sure everything (including a torch) is to hand so you can easily make yourself a hot drink during the night if necessary. Remove wet clothing and put on dry gear. Breakfast should, where possible, be a leisurely affair, and if conditions are kind it is a good idea to turn your sleeping bag inside out and air it over the ridge or a length of paracord.

As with pitching, striking camp should be done methodically. Clean your pans, wipe mud from the groundsheet, and make sure everything is packed in its correct place. If you dug a latrine or grease pit, back-fill them and replace turves. In wet weather, leave one tent standing until everything is packed away. If you are away for more than one night and you got wet the previous day, ensure you always have a set of dry clothing for use in camp, even if this means putting wet clothing on each morning.

Finally, when everything is packed away and you are ready to leave, cast your eyes carefully over the site to make sure nothing has been left. Within 24hrs of you leaving there should be nothing to indicate that anyone has camped.

# 6 Mountain navigation

Of all the skills of mountaincraft, it is undoubtedly that of navigation which has the greatest impact on mountain safety. Indeed, something in the order of 85% of all mountain accidents can be attributed to an initial error in navigation. Over the years I have found that the greatest problem in teaching navigation is people's prejudices – they think navigation is going to be complicated and feel they must be doing it wrong when they find that, in all honesty, the techniques themselves are simple.

As with other skills, you won't become an accurate navigator by reading a book. You must go out and practise in a realistic setting. I have room here only to give an overview of the major techniques. If you wish to find out more about navigation there are several relevant books mentioned in *section 11*.

Navigation should be, and can be, fun! If you find it a chore – if you become a slave to your navigation – you are not going about it in the right way. Skilled navigation should enhance the pleasures of the mountains, not detract from them. A common mistake is to think that navigation is the art of never getting lost. It is not! It is the art of working out where you are when you think you are lost. Perhaps the best way to put this in perspective is to say that a skilled navigator will never get lost although he may often be temporarily mislocated!

# Types of map

By far the most important piece of navigation equipment, a map, is simply a picture of the ground – nothing more, nothing less. In order to use it to navigate accurately, this picture needs to show as much relevant detail as possible, and for our purposes it is the terrain – the shape of the land – which is most important. The best maps are those made by the Ordnance Survey, both the Landranger series at a scale of 1:50,000 and the Pathfinder and Outdoor Leisure Series at a scale of 1:25,000. Specialist mountain maps (such as Harvey maps) are also extremely useful. Ideally you should be able to alternate between different maps without any problem. The Landranger and Harvey maps are useful when following good paths or definite ridges. If you are crossing trackless or more complex terrain, the extra detail shown on the 1:25,000 scale maps makes them indispensable.

Whatever type you use, do not forget that a map is out of date as soon as it is published. A map is a static thing whereas the landscape is dynamic. Forestry, in particular, changes at an alarming rate, and there may have been other changes which occurred after the map was surveyed. The only thing which does not change radically is the shape of the land – the terrain – so it is the shape of the land which becomes the most important consideration when you navigate.

It is a matter of personal choice whether you buy a standard map or a more expensive laminated, water-proof map. If you buy a standard map you must protect it from the elements in some way, even if this is only by placing it in a plastic bag.

## Types of compass

Compasses come in all manner of shapes and sizes, only a few of which are ideal for use in the mountains. Although you may be able to work out a rough direction from a small button compass, it is

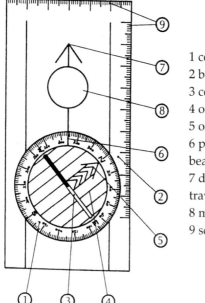

1 compass housing
2 base plate
3 compass needle
4 orientation lines
5 orientation arrow
6 point at which
   bearings are read
7 direction-of-
   travel arrow
8 magnifying lens
9 scales

*Figure 20: The orienteering compass*

not really accurate enough for our purposes. What is needed is an orienteering or protractor compass (*figure 20*). This will allow you to measure and follow bearings with great accuracy.

The orienteering compass comprises two major parts: the base plate and the compass housing. The base plate is a rectangle of clear plastic with scales along the front and one side. These scales can be in centimetres, although it is useful to have a set of Romer Scales in which the conversion from map distance to ground distance is done for you. Although Romer Scales are usually only found on the larger compasses, it is possible to buy these scales separately and these can be extremely useful. The base plate should be at least 10cms long, and should have a magnifying lens. Compasses with smaller base plates in which the magnifying lens is absent are available, but these are not recommended for serious mountain use.

Engraved on the base plate are a number of lines running parallel to the sides, the central one of which has an arrow, the Direction of Travel (or DOT) Arrow, at its front end and intersects the rim of the compass housing at its rear end. It is from this point that you read and set your bearings (*see below*).

The compass housing is a liquid filled capsule containing a magnetic needle, one end of which is red (the north-seeking end), the other, white. The rim of the housing is divided into segments (each of which represents 2° of arc), and is engraved with relevant figures and the relative positions of the cardinal points (north, south, east, and west). The base of the housing is engraved with a series of parallel lines (the orienting lines), the central two of which are joined together to form an arrow (the orienting arrow). The tip of the arrow points to the north position on the housing.

Although this is the basic type of orienteering compass, other versions are available. For example, the mirror compass has a hinged lid which covers the housing, the inside of which contains a mirror engraved with a fine line. When open, there is a mark on the cover at the top of the line, and it is possible to site on a feature or object and adjust the mirror in such a way that you can read the bearing at the same time. While this is undoubtedly a useful feature allowing you to follow and read bearings on the ground with considerable accuracy, there are two major disadvantages: firstly, few mirror compasses have base plates large enough to contain magnifying lenses or Romer scales, and secondly, it is very easy to get your bearings 180° wrong!

Better is the optical sighting compass, in which the compass housing has been extended to make room for a lens and prism, and the compass needle has been replaced by a complex wheel. By sighting through the lens and using a hair-line on the prism, you can take and follow bearings extremely accurately. However, the complexity of the needle on some models makes it fractionally more difficult to calculate accurate bearings from the map. Increasingly available and coming down in price are electronic GPS compasses. These expensive hi-tech gadgets can be useful in the hands of experienced navigators when used in conjunction with existing skills. However, they should not be seen as a shortcut to accurate navigation, and will only be of limited use to people learning the craft.

## Map skills

The most important skill in mountain navigation is the ability not just to read, but to interpret the map. There is a quantum difference between these two skills. Map reading is what you do when you drive from Dartmoor to the Cairngorms; map interpretation is what you do when caught in poor visibility on Dartmoor or the Cairngorms. Successful map interpretation requires you to look at your map in great detail. This is where the magnifying lens of your compass comes in handy. It is fair to say that the vast majority of people have no conception of the amount of detail shown on a map.

Maps are drawn to a particular scale. A scale of 1:25,000 simply means that one unit of measurement on the map is equal to 25,000 units of measurement on the ground. An easy way to judge scale is to ignore the final three digits, change the : to = (i.e. 1=25) and work from millimetres to metres (i.e. 1mm equals 25m). A further way to get an impression of scale is via the grid lines, the series of parallel lines which divide the map into squares. No matter what the scale of the map, the grid lines are always 1 km apart on the ground.

By quoting its position relative to the grid lines (through a grid reference), it is possible to describe the location of any feature anywhere in the country. The procedure is described in the key of every Ordnance

Survey map. Each grid line has a two figure reference number, and by quoting the reference number of the grid line to the left of the feature (e.g. 27) followed by the reference number of the grid line below the feature (e.g. 86) you can locate the feature to within a one kilometre square (e.g. 2786).

If you wish to be more accurate, you can estimate how many tenths of a square the feature is from the left line (e.g. 274) and how many tenths of a square above the lower line (e.g. 863), which locates the feature to within a 100 metre square (e.g. 274863). You could also estimate hundredths of a square to give an eight figure reference if that amount of accuracy is required. This would locate the feature to within a ten metre square. These references are unique for the map but will be repeated at 100 kilometre intervals across the country. If this is a problem, quote either the map number or, more correctly, the grid letters which are to be found in the map's key.

In order to allow us to interpret our picture of the ground, map makers use a series of symbols (conventional signs) in an attempt to make things clearer. It will be helpful if we think of these symbols as falling into one of five categories. The first category of conventional sign is symbols for things that aren't there including "Site of Battle" and "European Constituency Boundary" – not very useful when trying to locate yourself in the middle of a misty moor! We can ignore all of these symbols bar one – the spot height. This is simply a dot on the map with a surveyed height. Although there is nothing to indicate its presence on the ground, by comparing two adjacent spot heights it is possible to work out the aspect of slope (i.e. which way a slope faces). This can obviously be extremely important!

The second category of conventional sign is area symbols. These include areas of woodland (deciduous, coniferous or mixed), water, bog, boulders, loose rock, etc. They also include different vegetation types (rough pasture, heathland, bracken, etc.). Whilst you will not be able to navigate accurately using only these symbols, they can be very useful when route planning, and you may be able to gauge progress as you pass from one area to another.

The third category is pinpoint symbols (trig points, small pools, isolated sheep shelters, etc.). Many people will tell you that these are the most useful symbols as you can identify your position accurately by them. After all, if there is only one trig point shown on the map and you are standing by a trig point, you know precisely where you are. However, I feel that pinpoint symbols are of limited usefulness for one simple reason: they are so small relative to the landscape that you stand a good chance of missing them in misty conditions, especially if you are not sure precisely where you are in the first place! The next category of conventional sign – linear features – is far more useful.

Linear features comprise anything which is elongated (roads, rivers, field boundaries, etc.). If you are not sure precisely where you are and you notice from the map that there is a linear feature which lies roughly across your path, you have a fair chance of hitting it if you walk towards it. Granted you still do not know precisely where you are, but by following the linear feature (using it as a handrail), you may well come to another feature which you can use to relocate yourself.

Finally, we come to the most important category of them all – contour lines. It is these that show you the shape of the land, and it is the shape of the land which is the most important consideration when you are navigating in the mountains. Unfortunately, this is where many people switch off because they believe interpreting the contour lines to be difficult. This is not so. You only need to understand two basic principles and recognise three basic patterns to be able to interpret any landscape shape anywhere in the world.

A contour line is usually defined as a line which joins points of equal height. This does not really help us. Think, instead, of contour lines being imaginary paths (like sheep tracks) which wend their way through the mountains never gaining nor losing height. All these paths are equally spaced, so the difference in height between one line and the next (and the next and the next) remains constant across the map. This height difference is known as the vertical interval. The vertical interval on 1:25,000 and 1:50,000 OS maps in mountain areas is 10 metres. Because these lines represent differences in height, the closer they are together, the steeper must be the slope (see figure 21).

When these contour paths run across a smooth slope, they appear as smooth lines on the map, but when they come to a valley or a spur, they have to curve around the head of the valley or the front of the spur thus showing as a V or U shaped pattern

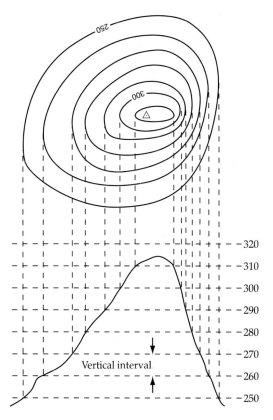

*Figure 21: Contour lines and the vertical interval*

on the map. Thus more or less straight lines
represent more or less smooth slopes, whereas V or
U shapes represent valleys or spurs. If a contour
line joins itself to form a circle, the path must go
round and round in circles, and the pattern must

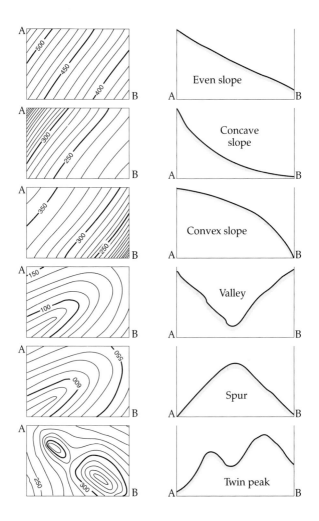

*Figure 22: Contour patterns and landscape shapes*

therefore represent either a dome shaped mountain or a rounded basin (*see figure 22*).

Contour patterns mimic the landscape they represent. Wide, rounded, flowing contour patterns show a wide, rounded, flowing landscape; sharp, angular contour patterns show a sharp, angular landscape. Moreover, a single squiggle on a single contour line represents a similarly shaped squiggle on the ground. If you are working from a 1:25,000 scale map and there is a 1mm squiggle on only one contour line, it represents a landscape feature which is at least 25m wide and up to 10m deep. Ask yourself whether this would be of significance in 20m visibility!

In order to interpret the contour patterns accurately, you need to know the aspect of slope. This is usually quite easy to work out as some of the contour lines will have the height they represent printed on them. Even if you can see only one contour marked in this way you can work out the aspect of slope because the figures on contours are always printed the right way up (i.e. with the top of the figure pointing towards the top of the slope). Alternatively, you can compare two adjacent spot heights. On those rare occasions where both these methods are impossible you can use other clues such as drainage. If you have a V or U shaped pattern with a river running down the middle of it, it is unlikely to be a spur!

One of the most useful but underutilised techniques is that of setting the map. This involves turning the map in such a way that everything on the map is in the same relative position on the ground. In other words, if you are looking in a southerly direction, your map should be upside down. With your map set correctly, features seen to your left will be to the left of your position on the map, and direction finding can be done simply by line of sight.

You can set your map in one of a number of ways. If you can recognise a number of features both on the ground and on the map, you can turn the map so that they all line up. Alternatively, if you are standing near a linear feature, you can turn the map so that the linear feature on the map runs in the same direction as the linear feature on the ground. Granted, you may be 180° out on occasions, but this should become immediately apparent once you start comparing other features. One further method makes use of the compass needle. Place your compass on the map so that the pivot of the needle lies on a north-south grid line. Now turn the map (not the compass) until the needle lies parallel to the grid line and the red (north-seeking) end of the needle points to the top of the map. Although this is not 100% accurate (for reasons which will become apparent later), it is usually sufficiently accurate to enable you to use the map effectively.

## Compass skills

In all but the worst conditions you should be able to navigate accurately using the map alone, especially if you learn to set it correctly and do everything by line of sight. However, there will be times, particularly in poor visibility, when you need a little help to travel in very accurate directions over precise distances. Having said this, I cannot overemphasise the fact that it is your map interpretation skills which are by far the most important. Compass skills and time and distance estimation are purely additional techniques which help to minimise errors. They are not the be all and end all of navigation. Indeed, you can be the best compass navigator in the world, able to calculate and follow bearings to within a second of arc, but unless you can relate all this information on to a map you will get lost!

The most common use of the compass is that of taking and following bearings. A bearing is simply the angle between two imaginary straight lines, one going from where you are to north, the other going from where you are to where you want to go. The convention in navigation is that bearings are always measured in a clockwise direction (i.e. in degrees east of north). To calculate an accurate grid bearing (i.e. from the map) you must be able to identify your current position and your proposed destination accurately on the map.

Once you have done this, place your compass on the map so that one side of the base plate lines up precisely between these two points, with the DOT Arrow pointing in the direction you wish to travel. If you are heading towards a feature which is quite large (e.g. a mountain pool), head towards the middle of it. If you are leaving from a feature which is large, choose a definite point from which to leave it and line up the side of the baseplate with this precise position.

When you are satisfied that the base plate is as accurately positioned as possible, keep it firmly in

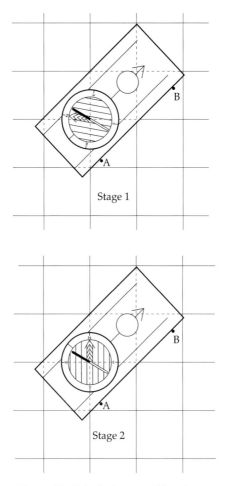

Figure 23: Calculating a grid bearing

position and turn the compass housing until the orientation lines lie parallel with the north-south grid lines and the orientation arrow points towards the top of the map. Double check that the DOT Arrow and the orientation arrow are pointing in the right direction and the side of the base plate is still lined up accurately between the two points. Once you have done this you have measured the angle and can remove the compass from the map *(figure 23)*.

Now we come to a slight complication for, in order to use this information on the ground, you need to alter your bearing slightly. The problem is that you have measured the angle with respect to grid north (the position towards which the grid lines point). If there were grid lines running across the countryside you could simply line up the orientation lines with the grid lines and follow the direction indicated by the Direction of Travel Arrow. But, of course, there are not. The only other lines which can be used are the lines of magnetic force as shown by your compass needle. The problem is that grid north and magnetic north are at different locations (the difference being known as the magnetic variation), so you must make an adjustment to compensate for this. The value of the magnetic variation is printed in the key of every OS map.

In the British Isles, magnetic north is currently to the west of grid north, and will be for some years to come. Because of this it is necessary to add the variation to the bearing shown on your compass *(see figure 24)*. When you turn the housing to do this, remember that each segment represents 2°. If you go abroad, you may find that the local

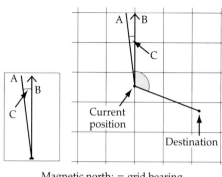

Magnetic north; = grid bearing
+magnetic variation

*Figure 24: magnetic variation. A=magnetic north;
B=grid north; C=magnetic variation*

magnetic variation is east of grid north. In this instance you would subtract the variation. It may help if you remember, when converting from a grid bearing to a magnetic bearing: east means least and west means best. Once you have adjusted for magnetic variation you will have converted your grid bearing into a magnetic bearing which can be used on the ground.

There is a definite technique when you come to follow your bearing on the ground. Hold the compass in front of you with the DOT arrow pointing directly away from you. Keep the compass as level as possible. Turn slowly around until the red end of the needle lies directly over the orientation arrow. Assuming that you have calculated your bearing accurately, the DOT arrow will now be pointing precisely to your destination. However, it is insufficient simply to walk in that direction. What you need to do is sight between the pivot of the needle and the DOT arrow and find an object which lies on course. This should be quite close by, and which you are going to reach. Avoid choosing objects which lie on the horizon.

Once done, put away your compass and walk to that object, avoiding any obstacles which lie in your way. When you arrive, repeat the procedure, and so on until you reach your destination. This may sound simple (in essence, it is), but it takes practice to do accurately in any conditions. The real art lies in choosing appropriate objects which remain recognisable as you approach them.

The art of successful compass navigation is being able to use the basic technique in all manner of situations. For example, you may be leaving a definite feature (say, a trig point) and heading across an apparently featureless moorland on which you are having difficulty in finding objects on which to sight. In this situation, a back bearing will save time and trouble.

Head off in roughly the right direction then, just before the trig point disappears from view, turn around until the white end of the compass needle lies directly over the orientation arrow. This is known as back bearing. Site along the DOT arrow in the normal way, and see if it points to the trig point. If it does, you are on course. If it does not, move yourself to the left or the right until it does (see figure 25). Back bearings also allow you to walk onto a bearing without having to visit the originating point.

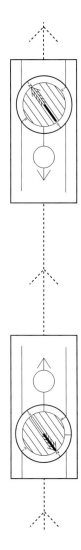

Another example is that of measuring the aspect of slope. This can be extremely helpful when, for example, searching for the correct descent gully on a curving ridge or cirque, or estimating a point from which to begin a descent. Take a bearing with the DOT arrow pointing down the gully or at right angles to the slope at the point at which you wish to begin the descent, and convert this to a magnetic bearing in the usual way. As you follow the top of the ridge or cirque, keep pointing the DOT arrow into the valley at right angles to the edge. When the red end of the needle lies over the orienteering arrow you have arrived at the correct point.

*Figure 25: top compass – back bearing. The white end of the needle lies over the orientation arrow, while the direction of travel arrow points to the position from which you have travelled. Bottom compass – standard bearing. The red (north-seeking) end of the needle lies over the orientation arrow, while the direction of travel arrow points towards the position for which you are making.*

Before descending, however, use your map interpretation skills to confirm that you are in the right position.

If you can measure the bearing between two points on the map (a grid bearing), you can also do the same when on the ground (a magnetic bearing). This can be an extremely useful way of locating your position, especially when you are standing on or by a linear feature. Let us say, for example, that you are standing on a narrow ridge. In front of you in the valley is a farmhouse which you can identify on the map. If you point the DOT arrow of your compass directly at the farmhouse, then turn the compass housing round until the orientation arrow lies directly beneath the red end of the needle, you have taken the magnetic bearing of the farmhouse. Assuming a westerly magnetic variation, if you now subtract the variation you will have converted this magnetic bearing into a grid bearing which you can now use on the map.

Place the compass on the map so that the front of one side of the base plate touches the farm. Without moving the compass housing, turn the whole compass around until the orientation arrow points to the top of the map and the orientation lines lie parallel with the north-south grid lines. Check to make sure the side of the base plate still touches the farm, in which case your position is where the same side of the base plate crosses the ridge on the map. The same technique can be used if you can see two features. Here you take a magnetic bearing on each and convert to grid. Your position will be where the two lines cross. Having said all this, if the visibility is good enough for you to see two features and you have set your map, you should be able to work out your position by line of sight and map interpretation!

All a compass does is show you the whereabouts of two invisible, imaginary straight lines, one running between two features of your choice, the other running from where you are to magnetic north. When using your compass, think in terms of straight lines. If you can work out a position or direction with straight lines on the map, you can work out the same position or direction with bearings on the ground.

## Estimating time

An accurate compass bearing will show you precisely in which direction you should travel. What it will not do is tell you how far you have been or how far you have yet to go. Particularly in bad weather conditions it is easy to lose all track of time and distance, so the ability to estimate how long it is going to take you to walk between two points can be extremely useful.

In its coarsest form, estimating time is useful when planning your route. Particularly when visiting a new area for the first time, it is useful to be able to glance at a map and work out whether a proposed route is going to be an easy dawdle or a strenuous yomp. Map distance and ground distance are two totally separate measurements in mountain areas because the map is flat whereas the ground is not. The ups and downs need to be taken into consideration.

The basic formula for calculating duration is known as Naismith's Rule. This is usually quoted as: **5 kph plus 30 minutes for every 300 metres of ascent.**

This is a good starting block for calculating how long a proposed walk will take. However, it is too unwieldy to be of much use during micro-navigation in poor visibility, so it is necessary to chunk it down into manageable portions. Additionally, I work on the basis that if you are concentrating hard on your navigation in bad conditions, you will probably be moving slightly slower than 5 kph, so I always use 4 kph as the baseline. When chunked down this equates to: **1.5 minutes per 100 metres plus 1 minute for every 10 metres of ascent.**

As the contour interval on most maps is 10 metres, you simply measure the horizontal distance using the scale or Romer on your compass baseplate, then add a minute for every uphill contour you cross. Generally speaking you can ignore descending contours unless the descent is very long or very steep, in which case add 1 minute for every second contour.

This baseline timing works well for me, but it will not necessarily work well for you as you may walk at a completely different pace. It is, however, a good starting block. Only you can decide what timing works for you – and you can only calculate your baseline through practical experience. You will also find that it varies slightly from day to day and depending upon the weather conditions, the load being carried, the severity of the terrain, and so on. With experience you should be able to adjust your time estimates accordingly.

## Estimating distance

If estimating time is useful, then having the ability to estimate distance is a must. In its most macroscopic form this will involve judging distances on the ground. This is extremely difficult to do and even experienced navigators will get it wrong most of the time! Far more useful (and, luckily, easier and more accurate) is estimating distance on a much smaller scale, and this is done by pace counting.

Before you are able to pace count, you need to calibrate your pace. What you need is a measured distance of 100 metres. Although this can easily be found by visiting you local leisure centre and using the 100 metres running track, this is not the best way to calibrate your pace because you will take fewer paces to travel 100 flat and level metres than you will to cross 100 metres of rough heathland. Unless you have a companion who can pace count accurately, you will need to borrow a surveyor's tape or use a 50m length of climbing rope to measure the distance. When you calibrate your pace, you count 1 step every time your left foot hits the ground. Neither exaggerate your pace nor walk in a group when you do this (if you walk in a group you will begin to affect each other's paces). Pace the distance three or four times and work out the average number of double paces you take to travel 100 metres.

This is an extremely useful figure. Let us assume that you take 65 paces per 100 metres and you are travelling a distance of 425 metres (as measured from the map) on a compass bearing in poor visibility. What you do not do is multiply 65 by 4.25! You pace count in terms of hundreds of metres rather than hundreds of paces. So pick up four pieces of straw, small pebbles, bits of grass, whatever comes to hand. Set off on your compass bearing and count your paces until you have reached 65. You now have travelled 100 metres, so throw away one of the pieces of straw (or whatever) and start counting your paces from one again.

In this way you do not have to do any complicated mental arithmetic, and by glancing at the things you have collected you can always tell how far you have left to go. In this example, when you throw away the final thing you know you should be only 25 metres from your destination. Even if you are 3 or 4 paces out per hundred metres, you will be less than 20 paces out when you reach your destination. With practice you can be very accurate indeed.

## Poor visibility navigation

Navigating in poor visibility should, in theory, be no more difficult than navigating in good conditions. However, confidence plays a big part and you may well feel waves of uncertainty pouring over you, especially if getting the right direction is critical. The best advice I can give is to remember the word KISS – which stands for Keep It Short and Simple. Each leg of navigation should be as short as you can possibly make it, certainly no more than 500 metres, even if this means heading to iffy points such as small squiggles on single contour lines. Try to get the feel of the terrain through your feet. Even on apparently level ridges and gently undulating plateaux it is possible to feel whether you are going uphill or down. Remember such information; it may be extremely useful.

Poor visibility navigation is an exercise in damage limitation. The further you go, the greater any compound error will be, so KISS! Double check your compass bearings by setting your map and seeing if the direction shown by the set map is the same as the direction shown by the compass. Work out timings and distances, and concentrate on what you are doing. Map interpret along the length of the leg to see if there is anything you can use to judge progress or give confidence that you are on route, look just before your destination to see if there is anything which will indicate you are nearing your objective, and look just beyond the point for which you are making to see if there is anything which will indicate that you have overshot.

When following a compass bearing you may find it difficult to find objects or features which lie directly on your route. If this happens, use your companions and leapfrog. Send a companion on in front until he is nearing the limit of visibility then sight on him and, by arm movements, move him to the left or right until he is standing directly on course. Signal for him to stop, then walk to him. If he also has a compass set to the same bearing you can walk past him so he can sight on you, and so on.

The best features to aim for are linear features which lie more or less across your course. If you aim for a precise point on such a feature (for example, a stream junction), you will undoubtedly reach the stream but unless you have been accurate with your compass work, you may not be able to see the junction. Sod's Law dictates that in this situation you will always turn the wrong way! To save this happening, deliberately aim off to one side so that when you reach the stream junction you know which way to turn.

Whenever possible use map interpretation combined with natural features to aid your navigation. Linear features can be used as handrails which lead you towards an objective. For example, let us use a scene where you are walking towards a small pool and the mist comes down. You see from your map that to your right is an area of forest, out of which issues a stream which leads to the pool. Why use a compass? It is far easier to turn half right and find the forest edge, walk along this until you come to the stream then follow the stream to the pool.

There may also be times when it is easier to approach your destination from a different direction, when, for example, there is a linear feature beyond it. Walk to the linear feature first (easy) then find some feature along it from where to reach your destination. This is known as using an attack point. Remember – KISS!

If the worst happens, don't panic! If, according to your pacing, timing and compass work, you should be at your destination, try doing a simple line search in which someone stays on the bearing whilst the other members of the party spread out in a line abreast, each person within sight of the next. The line then moves forwards along a standard bearing or backwards along a back bearing in the hope that the destination is nearby and will be within sight of one of the party. If you do not find it, you will have to relocate yourself as described later. Always keep someone on the original bearing as, if the worst comes to the worst, you can retrace your steps along a back bearing. If you lose the position of this bearing you will have lost all points of reference and relocating yourself will be that much more difficult.

## Night navigation

There are many similarities between poor visibility navigation and night navigation. The techniques remain the same (including KISS), as do many of the problems. Judging distance can be virtually impossible when all you can see are silhouettes, so try to use physical features such as breaks of slope to keep track of how far you have travelled. On a clear night there is nothing wrong with using a star as a feature to sight on, but make sure you can recognise it again. Because the stars move relative to the horizon, you should not follow the same star for more than about ten minutes at a stretch. Far more accurate if somewhat more time consuming is to leapfrog using pen torches to sight on.

Try to use map interpretation, handrails and attack points whenever possible, and if at all possible, allow your eyes to adapt to night vision. This will take at least 20 minutes to develop, and can be lost immediately if you turn on a torch. If there is insufficient light to see the map correctly, use a long-life bulb in your headtorch (this gives less light than standard or halogen bulbs) and close one eye so it remains dark adapted. Red light will not affect night vision, but it is pointless using a red filter over the lens of your torch because you will be unable to read the brown contour lines on your map!

## Relocation

There will inevitably come a time when you suddenly realise that you have absolutely no idea of where you are. This is when you need a methodical relocation technique. First and foremost, don't panic! Tell yourself that you are not lost. You must know where you are to within a few kilometres, even if you cannot pinpoint your position. You know where you started from and you know how long you have been walking, so that's a good start. You may even have a rough idea of the direction in which you have been travelling, and that can help as well. If you are standing by a definite feature, you are almost home and dry and should be able to work out your position by a process of elimination (see below), but let us work on the basis that you are standing in the middle of a featureless plateau and can see nothing but rocks, heather, and mist.

The worst thing you can do at this stage is to stick your nose in the map, simply because there is no way that the map can show you where you are. Don't look at a map for at least five minutes. Look around and try to get a feel for the area. Start by asking questions about the shape of the ground and the terrain. Are you high or low? Does the ground slope in any particular direction? What is the vegetation like?

Use all your senses – listen for water or the breeze in trees, smell the air, probe the mist to see if you can sense a cliff or something nearby. You may laugh, but try it and you will be amazed how much information you can pick up about your surroundings. Once you have worked out a rough location, look at your map to see if there is a linear feature in the area. If so, head towards it, taking great care if you are high and there are clifftops around. In winter, be aware of the dangers of cornices *(see page 207)* if there is any possibility that you may be walking towards the top of the crag.

If you have been following a bearing and you cannot find your destination, check to make sure the bearing was correct and that your compass has not been altered inadvertently during the journey. If the bearing is wrong, work out where the set bearing has put you. Once you have worked out a rough location, look at your map and see if there are any linear features in the area which would act as handrails. It is extremely unusual to find nothing.

Once you are standing by the linear feature (or any other feature for that matter) you are in a far better position to pinpoint your location. You may be able to do this simply by following the handrail to an obvious point. Alternatively you may find, having looked around and consulted your map, that you could be at any one of a number of locations. You should be able to distinguish one from the other by map interpretation or by measuring directions with your compass.

If this proves impossible, you need to find something on the map which is within two or three hundred metres of your most likely position. Walk on a compass bearing towards this, pacing the distance. If you arrive at the feature you now know with 100% certainty where you are. If you do not arrive at the feature after the paced distance, turn around and regain your original position using a back bearing. In this way you now know where you are not (!). By continuing the exercise from all possible points you should eventually be able to work out your precise position by a process of elimination.

## Route cards

It would be remiss of me not to mention route cards in a book about mountain safety. A route card is basically a list of grid references, bearings, timings, etc. which describe the route you are planning to follow when in the hills *(see figure 26)*. From a safety point of view, you can leave a copy of this with a responsible person so that, in the event of your non-return, a mountain rescue team can be called out and will know where to look for you.

Route cards tend to be a contentious subject. Many people dislike them because they believe they destroy the spontaneity of walking. However, I feel they have several benefits. For a start, to write a route card, you have to sit down with your map and plan the route. In doing this you get a good idea of the bare bones of the area you intend to visit. Secondly, it is far easier to work out accurate bearings etc. whilst sitting at a table than it is to do the same thing across the fold of a map in strong winds! Thirdly, if things do go wrong whilst you are out, all your navigational computations are to hand, and this is one less thing you have to worry about.

| DATE: | START POINT: | | | FINISH POINT: | | RETURN TIME: |
|---|---|---|---|---|---|---|
| FEATURE | GRID REF | M° | DIST (m) | HT ↑ (m) | Time (mins) | REMARKS |
| | | | | | | |
| | | | | | | |
| | | | | | | |
| | | | | | | |
| | | | | | | |
| | | | | | | |
| | | | | | | |

FRONT OF CARD

| SIZE OF PARTY: | (adults)+ | (children). | No of LEADERS |
|---|---|---|---|
| EQUIPMENT CARRIED: | | | |
| | | | |
| ESCAPE ROUTES: | | | |
| | | | |
| | | | |
| | | | |
| | | | |
| | | | |

*Figure 26: example of a blank route card*

I also believe that route cards need not destroy spontaneity. Let us assume you have made out a route card for a particular walk. You will undoubtedly start from the position intended, but during the first or second leg of navigation you decide to leave your planned route and make for a ridge which looks like it may have a good viewpoint. You then wander round the area, never actually on the route described – until something happens. If the unexpected occurs, you relocate yourself and head to the nearest point mentioned on your route card (if necessary, by walking on to a bearing *as described on page 159*), from which point life will become a little easier.

While I do not believe it is necessary to make out a formal route card every time you visit the mountains, I feel you would be well advised to if you are in charge of a group or walking by yourself.

# 7 Mountain weather

The prevailing weather conditions have a profound effect on your visits to the mountains, and unexpected changes in the weather can quickly turn a delightful day into a nightmare. It is essential, therefore, that you have a basic understanding of weather and the way in which it affects both the mountain environment and you.

To take an extreme example, freezing conditions will affect you directly by making you cold; they will also affect you indirectly by making the ground icy. More mundanely, perhaps, rain will affect you directly by making you wet; it will also affect you indirectly by making the ground wet and slippery, raising stream levels, and reducing visibility. But individual weather factors cannot be taken in isolation – it is the combination of weather conditions, of wind and wet and cold, which can be of vital importance.

Generally speaking, the higher you go the more extreme will become the weather. Mountains are always colder, wetter and windier than lowlands. If there is drizzle carried on a light breeze at sea level, there could well be torrential rain (or sleet) carried on gale force winds on the tops. Before visiting the mountains, therefore, it is essential to get an up-to-date, local weather forecast (or, at the very least, a good national forecast) and know how to modify it to mountain conditions.

To do this with any degree of accuracy, you should have a basic understanding of frontal systems, and a reasonable knowledge of the weather conditions associated with various airflows.

It is also important that you have some conception of the ways in which the mountains affect the weather and the weather affects the mountains. Even with a limited amount of weatherlore you should be able to recognise the onset of bad weather before it arrives, although it will take years of practice before you can forecast it with any accuracy. After all, mountains make their own weather and even the experts get it wrong!

## Airstreams

The British Isles experience some of the most complex weather patterns in the world. This is due largely to the fact that the islands are affected by six major airstreams, each of which comes from a different direction and carries a different type of weather (*figure 27*). If you know which airstream is affecting the country at any given time, you will have a good idea of the expected weather.

The most prevalent airstream is the Polar maritime, which affects the country for about 35% of the year. Coming in from the west or north-west, it brings cool temperatures and heavy, often prolonged showers. If there is an area of low pressure (see later) in the North Atlantic, this airstream can loop around below it to arrive from the south-west, in which case it will bring warmer but cloudy weather with occasional squally showers.

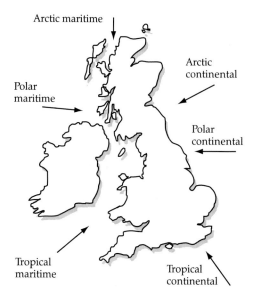

*Figure 27: air flows*

The second most common airstream is Tropical maritime which comes in from the south-west. In summer this usually brings warm temperatures but is often associated with low cloud over western hills. In winter it often brings mild, moist, cloudy conditions.

Next comes Polar continental air which blows in from the east bringing hot, hazy days in summer and bitter, Siberian conditions in winter. Also coming out of the east is Arctic continental air. This only occurs in winter when it brings extreme conditions including blizzards and sustained frosts. Arctic Maritime airstreams originate in the Arctic Ocean and come down from the north bringing unseasonably cold spells in summer together with frequent, often squally showers. During the winter months this airstream can be responsible for heavy snowfall in the mountains.

Finally, blowing up from the south is the Tropical Continental airstream which only occurs in summer, and then rarely. It brings extremely hot, heatwave temperatures together with a high risk of thunder.

## Temperature

Generally speaking, the higher you climb, the colder it becomes. When air encounters the mountains it is forced to rise. As it does so it encounters less atmospheric pressure which allows it to expand, and as a consequence of this, it cools. The rate at which the temperature decreases with height is known as the Lapse Rate, and owing to their location, the British Isles have some of the highest Lapse Rates in the world.

The value of the Lapse Rate is not constant but depends upon the amount of water vapour in the air. In general terms, the more moist the air, the lower the Lapse Rate. The average Lapse Rate in Britain is of the order of 2°C per 300 metres. During windy conditions (or if the air is particularly dry), this can increase to 3°C per 300 metres. On the other hand, if the air is saturated with moisture the Lapse Rate may fall to below 1.5°C per 300 metres. As a rule of thumb, the Lapse Rate will be high on windy days and low when the clouds are way down over the tops, and will slowly decrease with height. Additionally, because cold air cannot hold so much water vapour as warm air, the average Lapse Rate is lower in winter than in summer.

A further effect of the Lapse Rate is that of the Föhn Effect *(see figure 28)*. As the air hits the mountains, it rises, expands and cools. Because cool air cannot hold so much water vapour as warm air, it may eventually become saturated. If this happens it is said to have reached the Dew Point and any further cooling or expansion will result in condensation of the vapour into clouds or even rain *(see page 185)*.

As the water vapour content of the air increases so there will be a corresponding decrease in Lapse

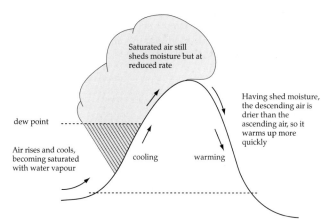

*Figure 28: Lapse rate and the Föhn Effect*

Rate. As the air crosses the mountains it will obviously lose some of its water content in the form of clouds, drizzle or rain, so when it begins to descend on the far side it will be drier.

Because the Lapse Rate becomes greater the drier the air, this descending air will warm up at a faster rate than it cooled down (the Föhn Effect), and this can result in the air of the leeside of the British mountains being 1°C to 2°C warmer than it was on the windward side. In larger mountain ranges such as the European Alps, the temperature differences can be even more marked. Indeed, the turbulent Föhn wind in the French Alps is often the cause of wet avalanches.

The general effects of the Lapse Rate can sometimes be turned on their head leading the valley floors to be colder than the tops. When this occurs there is said to be a temperature inversion *(see figure 29)*. These usually occur on windless nights when dense, cold air flows down the mountainside and collects in a layer in the valleys.

As it flows down the slopes it will also collect in any sheltered basins on the way forming frost hollows. The effect can be marked, and temperatures in frost hollows can be in the order of 5°C colder than those on the open slopes. In the more sheltered valleys, the cold air can be several hundreds of metres thick and can result in dense fog, heavy dews and hard frosts. Most inversions will burn off shortly after the sun hits them in the morning. However, they can persist for days in deep, narrow valleys which rarely get the sun.

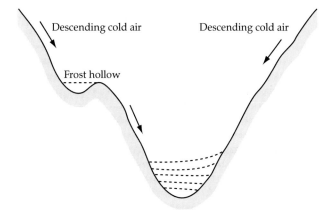

*Figure 29: temperature inversion*

## Wind

Days of total calm are rare in the mountains. Even if there is no appreciable breeze in the valleys, there will usually be a noticeable wind somewhere on the tops. This is due to a number of factors. As a general rule, the higher you climb, the stronger will be the force of the wind.

Wind speeds on general weather forecasts usually refer to the predicted speeds at sea level. This is one of the many reasons that you should always try to get a local forecast relevant to the mountains. On the better of these they will give you wind speeds and directions at various heights. Many people underestimate the effect of the wind on the mountains. For example, a force 4 wind will rip an open map to shreds whilst a force 6 will make sighting on bearings difficult. A gust of force 7 will blow you over, and if you get caught in a steady force 8 or 9 you will be unable to make any progress except, perhaps, by crawling. Further details are given in the Beaufort Wind Scale in *figure 30*.

| Force | Forecast | Speed | Effects |
|---|---|---|---|
| 0 | calm | <1 | Water mirror-calm; smoke rises straight up; no effect on fresh snow. |
| 1 | light | 2-5 | Wind just discernible; smoke drifts fractionally; no effect on fresh snow. |
| 2 | light | 5-10 | Light vegetation trembles; ripples on open water; no effect on fresh snow. |
| 3 | light | 10-20 | Heather moves; small waves on open water; slight surface drift of fresh snow. |
| 4 | moderate | 20-30 | Small branches move; dry grass lifted on wind; spindrift up to 1m high. |
| 5 | fresh | 30-40 | Small trees sway; difficult to pitch tent; widespread drifting of fresh snow. |
| 6 | strong | 40-50 | Walking requires extra effort; large branches move; spindrift above 2m. |
| 7 | strong | 50-60 | Large trees sway; danger of being blown over; near blizzard conditions. |
| 8 | gale | 60-75 | Walking impossible with large rucksack; small branches break; blizzard. |
| 9 | gale | 75-90 | Crawling difficult; standing impossible; large branches break. |
| 10 | storm | 90-105 | Body dragged along by wind; trees uprooted. |

*Figure 30: Beaufort Wind Scale*

The easiest way to understand the ways in which mountains affect the wind is to imagine that there is a ceiling above which the air cannot travel. Although air flows across the sea or the lowlands without much hindrance, friction with the ground will cause the surface winds to be lighter than higher winds. When the air reaches the mountains it is forced by rising ground to pass through a progressively smaller gap, and this causes it to speed up in a similar manner to water passing over a weir *(figure 31)*. If the peak is isolated, the wind will tend to flow around it giving the highest wind speeds on the shoulders of the hill *(figure 32)*.

The Lapse Rate also has an Effect on the way in which the air behaves when it reaches a mountain barrier. If the rate is high (as it often is on windy days), the air is unstable and will try to climb over the barriers. Conversely, if the rate is low (when the air is saturated as in low cloud), the air is unstable and will try to flow around barriers.

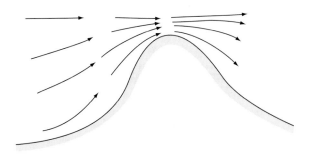

*Figure 31: Effect of high ground on wind*

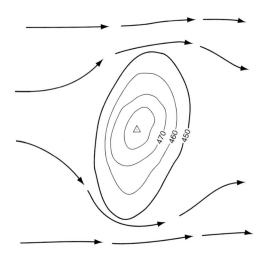

*Figure 32: Wind speed increase over shoulders*

If there is a valley or a col lying in the same direction as the wind, this will act like a funnel which causes the air to speed up. If the valley curves around, the wind trapped within it will follow the line of the valley *(figure 33)*.

Most mountain walkers will be familiar with the problems caused by turbulence. In its simplest form, this will simply be gusting winds. However, there are other forms of turbulence worth considering. Any sudden sharp change in the angle of slope will have an effect on the wind. This is particularly noticeable on sharp ridges and cliff edges. If the wind is blowing across the break of slope, the main

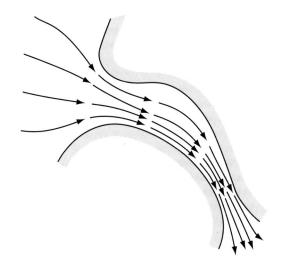

*Figure 33: topography causing change of wind direction*

*Figure 34: leeside eddies and null points*

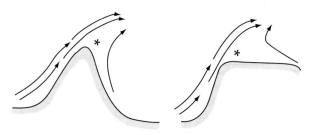

Eddy formed by ridge                    Eddy formed by scarp edge

✻ Indicates approximate position of possible null point

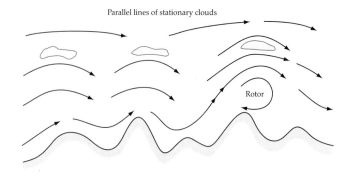

*Figure 35: rotor*

wind will continue in its original direction for some time, and this will cause a leeside eddy *(figure 34)* – a weaker wind blowing in the opposite direction. This often results in a null point – a corridor of calm – along which it is possible to walk out of the wind. However, null points are neither constant nor continuous; when using them you should beware unexpected gusts especially when approaching the tops of gullies or changes in direction.

In areas where the wind has blown across a series of parallel ridges it can begin to flow in waves. Conditions such as this are often recognisable by parallel lines of stationary clouds. If these waves are large or extensive, the wind can become extremely turbulent and can sometimes form a rotor in which a gust comes unexpectedly from the opposite direction *(figure 35)*.

Something people are far more aware of nowadays

| Wind speed kph | Ambient temperature (C) | | | | | | |
|---|---|---|---|---|---|---|---|
| 0 | 12 | 8 | 4 | 0 | -4 | -8 | -12 |
| 10 | 8 | 5 | 0 | -4 | -8 | -13 | -17 |
| 20 | 4 | 0 | -5 | -10 | -15 | -21 | -26 |
| 30 | 0 | -3 | -8 | -14 | -20 | -25 | -31 |
| 40 | -1 | -5 | -11 | -17 | -23 | -29 | -35 |
| 50 | -2 | -6 | -12 | -18 | -25 | -31 | -37 |
| 60 | -4 | -7 | -13 | -19 | -26 | -32 | -39 |
| 70 | -4 | -7 | -14 | -20 | -27 | -32 | -40 |

*Figure 36: wind-chill chart*

is wind-chill. This is simply the chilling effect of the wind. Contrary to popular opinion, however, the wind does not have to be strong to have a high wind-chill effect. Indeed, the greatest effects are at slower speeds, as can be seen from *figure 36*. Although this gives a fair indication of likely effects, rain will increase the temperature drops if allowed to penetrate clothing *(see page 15)* or fall on exposed flesh. In the same way that mountains are colder and windier than the lowlands, they are also wetter. The main reason for this has already been explained when describing the mechanisms of Lapse Rate and the Föhn Effect.

## Precipitation

As air flows across the sea it picks up vast quantities of water vapour. When it reached the mountains it is forced to rise, expanding and cooling as it does so.

The cooler and less dense the air, the less water vapour it can hold, so there will eventually come a time when the air becomes saturated and any excess water vapour will begin to condense into droplets. The point at which it does this is known as the dew point. Above this point, water will continue to condense forming either cloud, drizzle, or rain. If it is already raining (caused, perhaps, by a frontal system – see below), the rain will become heavier.

On the leeside of the mountains the air descends, compresses and warms up. It can therefore hold increasing amounts of water vapour and this can result in a rain shadow. The leeward sides of mountains are therefore often drier than the windward sides. However, this rain shadow effect is often negated during windy weather as strong winds will drive the rain on over the mountains.

In addition to the rainfall caused by topography, there is also rainfall associated with frontal systems. Mountains form an effective barrier to these systems and will slow them down. Therefore any frontal rain will tend to last longer over mountain areas than it will over the lowlands. To put all this in perspective, modern estimates put the average annual rainfall on the summit of Snowdon at twice that of Capel Curig (12kms east and 900 metres lower), and six times that of the Cheshire Plain (90kms east and 1,000 metres lower).

There are two other forms of precipitation which will have a dramatic effect in the mountains. The first is hail. This is almost always associated with cumulonimbus clouds and often with thunderstorms. Although light hail may not cause any problems, being caught in a hailstorm can be a painful experience as some stones can have edges sharp enough to cut when driven on a strong wind. Few storms last long, so the best idea is to find some shelter and sit it out.

The other important form of precipitation is snow which will obviously affect the mountains in many ways. Most rain falling on Britain starts life as snow at high altitude, and if the temperature is cold enough, it will reach the ground. As it descends and meets air above freezing point, it will begin to melt, first clumping together to form large flakes, then turning to sleet and finally to rain. Generally speaking, the warmer the temperature, the larger

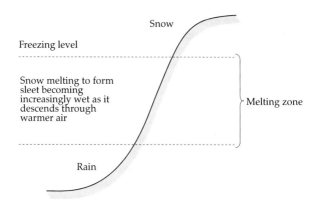

*Figure 37: the melting zone*

the snowflakes. This melting zone may be over 250 metres in depth, which means that the snow line is not necessarily the same as the freezing level *(figure 37)*. It is also worth noting that because of the effects of variable Lapse Rate and the cooling effect of rain, the snow line (and the freezing level) can drop by a significant amount during the day. This means that the damp path you followed in the morning can be snow covered and icy by the time you return in the afternoon.

The snow that you will meet on the mountains will not be uniform in consistency, but will vary from powder, through something resembling sugar, to stuff like porridge and finally consolidated snow which is almost as hard as ice. Different types of snow bring with them their own set of problems and delights. As I have mentioned before, your initial winter expeditions should be with an experienced companion or a suitably qualified instructor.

When recounting their experiences on the hill, people frequently talk about white out conditions when, in fact, they mean thick mist. A true white out can only occur in misty conditions when there is snow both in the air and on the ground. Under these circumstances everything becomes white – there is no differentiation between airborne snow and lying snow. Your companions will appear to float, and it will be impossible to tell what is up and what is down. Whilst conditions such as this are rare south of the Scottish Border, they can occur almost anywhere *(see page 218)*.

A further potential problem is that of spindrift or

airborne snow crystals which can cause a significant reduction in visibility. These get everywhere! It need not be snowing for there to be spindrift – even a slight breeze will pick up unconsolidated snow crystals. Given a slight breeze, the colder it is and the more recently it has snowed, the more likely you are to encounter spindrift. If spindrift is carried on a significant wind you can have white out conditions without there being any snow falling.

Arguably the worst condition you will ever meet on the hill is that of blizzard. This is more than just windy weather and falling snow, it is a snowstorm in every sense of the word. If it is really cold (which it is likely to be), the snow crystals can be so fine that they make breathing difficult or even impossible when facing the wind. In any case, windblown snow is painfully abrasive; trying to walk into the teeth of a blizzard is like walking into a sand-blasting machine! If blizzard conditions (snowfall and high winds) are forecast or suspected, stay off the hill. If the weather is working up to these conditions, retreat early, even if you have to descend into the wrong valley. If you get caught in blizzard conditions, seek shelter *(see also section 10)*.

## Frontal systems

The airstreams which affect the British Isles each have different characteristics. When different types of air meet, particularly warm air and cold air, they form swirling areas of instability which lead to depressions (areas of low pressure) and anticyclones (areas of high pressure). These are shown on weather maps by isobars (lines joining points of

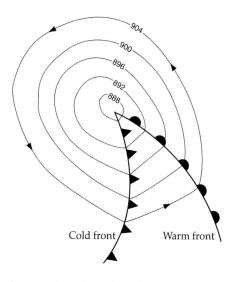

*Figure 38: a frontal system*

equal pressure). In the same way that contours show the steepness of the terrain, isobars show the steepness of the pressure differences. Because air always tries to reach equilibrium, it flows from areas of high pressure and tries to fill areas of low pressure. The closer the isobars are together, the greater the pressure difference, and therefore the stronger the wind in that area. In the most general terms, depressions bring unsettled weather whereas anticyclones bring settled conditions. Air flows in an anticlockwise direction around a depression and in a clockwise direction around an anticyclone.

Associated with areas of low pressure are frontal

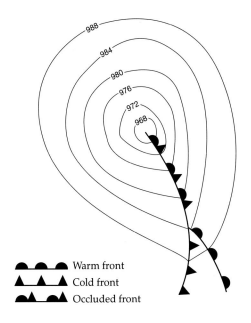

*Figure 39: an occluded front*

systems. A front is simply the junction between air masses of different temperatures. If warm air is advancing the junction is termed a warm front; if cold air is advancing it is known as a cold front. These fronts usually occur together in a depression, radiating out from the centre with the warm front preceding the cold, the whole system moving across the Atlantic in an easterly direction at speeds of between 20kph and 80kph *(see figure 38)*. However, cold fronts move faster than warm fronts so the two will eventually merge. When this happens the front

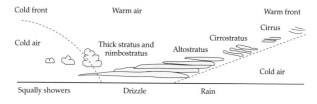

*Figure 40: section through a frontal system*

is said to be occluded *(see figure 39).*

In theory, there is a definite sequence of events as a frontal system passes over a mountain range. The arrival and passage of the system can be seen in terms of the development of different cloud types and changes in wind direction *(see figure 40).* Indeed, the recognition of different cloud types should be seen as an essential skill. However, because mountains affect the weather in so many ways, this sequence may well be affected in detail and the differences and changes may not be so clear cut as described below. Nevertheless, a knowledge of the sequence can be extremely useful in predicting possible changes in the weather.

The first signs of an approaching frontal system are usually long streaks of high cirrus clouds (Mare's Tails) which begin to appear up to 24 hours before the arrival of the warm front. The wind slowly increases and backs (changes its heading in an anti-clockwise direction), and the high clouds continue to develop into continuous wispy sheets of cirro-stratus which cast a halo around the sun or moon, and eventually into lower bands of grey altostratus which may herald the start of the rain. The wind continues to back and strengthen, and the nearer the front, the lower and darker the clouds. These eventually develop into continuous sheets of stratus and nimbostratus which often give continuous rain.

As the warm front passes, the wind suddenly decreases and veers (changes its heading in a clockwise direction), and the temperature rises. In lowland areas the clouds now start to disperse, but in the mountains they tend to hang around giving drizzle and poor visibility. As the cold front nears, the wind begins to increase again and cumulus clouds begin to form (although these may be hidden by lower clouds in mountain areas).

As the cold front passes, the wind veers again, the temperature plummets, and there may be sudden squally showers. The clouds now start to disperse giving way to clearing skies and showery weather.

If the fronts have occluded (as is common in the British mountains), the sequence remains essentially the same except that there will be no warm sector, the weather jumping straight from the band of rain to clearing skies with a marked veering of the wind.

## Lightning

Although lightning is not a major cause of mountain accidents, it does kill two or three people each year. A basic understanding of the principles involved is therefore useful knowledge.

In simple terms, lightning is an electrical discharge

from the atmosphere. During a thunderstorm, the clouds become charged with electricity which then arcs or jumps to earth causing a flash of lightning. Because electricity takes the line of least resistance, it tends to arc across the shortest possible distance and therefore almost invariably strikes the most prominent feature in its locality.

A lightning strike is rather like dropping a raw egg onto a concrete floor from a height of about ten metres: it doesn't just break, it splatters all over the place! When the electricity from the cloud strikes the ground, it does not simply disappear; it spreads out from the strike in a series of ground currents, each one following the line of least resistance in an attempt to go to ground as quickly as possible. These lines of least resistance tend to be damp cracks and gullies, and if there are any breaks or obstacles such as caves or overhanging rocks, the electricity will arc across them in the same way as the electricity arcs in a car's spark plug.

There will usually be plenty of advance warning of an approaching thunderstorm for you should be able to see and hear it coming. As it gets closer, you will also be able to feel it! Your skin will prickle, your hair may literally stand on end, and any local projections may begin to glow with the bluish light of St Elmo's fire. Perhaps more alarming, metal objects such as ice axes may spark and hum.

Because strikes tend to be concentrated on the most prominent features, there is a zone around these which is less prone to strikes. Although these zones have been described as safe areas, the

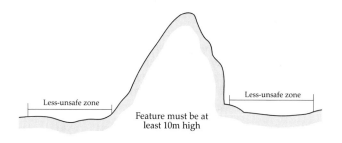

Less-unsafe zone

Less-unsafe zone

Feature must be at
least 10m high

*Figure 41: less-unsafe zone*

terminology is misleading and it would be better to
think of them in terms of less-unsafe zones. These
zones lie around features more than 7 metres high
and have a diameter roughly equal to the height of
the feature *(see figure 41)*.

When faced with an approaching thunderstorm,
your priority should be to move away from
exposed ridges, mountain tops and any prominent
features and get into one of these less-unsafe zones.
Try to find a relatively flat, open area within the
zone, sit down on the driest object you can find
(rucksack, rope, etc.), pull your legs up to your chin
and clasp your hands around your knees. Although
you have minimised the chances of a direct strike,
there is still the problem of ground currents, so try
to keep minimum contact with the ground and
resist the temptation to lean back on your hands. If
you do lean back and you are hit by a ground
current, the electricity will pass through every
major organ in your body. If you crouch or sit as

described, however, a ground current strike will only pass through your legs.

By now it will be pouring with rain (or hailing) and there will be a great temptation to find shelter. On no account should you seek shelter in gullies or fissures as these are the most likely paths for the ground currents. Similarly, sheltering in shallow caves or beneath overhanging rocks can be extremely dangerous as, if met by a ground current, these can act like spark-plug gaps and you could be severely burned by electric arc. It may be prudent to place metal objects such as ice axes to one side, but they should not be discarded as they may be needed for a safe retreat. In any case, contrary to popular belief, they do not attract lightning any more than you do!

Finally, give some thought to secondary effects. For example, if you have taken all the precautions outlined above, it is unlikely that a ground current will kill you. However, it may stun you with potentially serious consequences if you are on steep ground. If you are scrambling on an exposed ridge with no possibility of retreat, try to find a flat area below the crest and sit it out. Moreover, during thunderstorms there is an increased chance of stonefall. Not only can lightning shatter rocks and boulders by vaporising the water trapped within them, but the noise and vibration from thunder can topple already unstable boulders.

## Forecast sources

Because the weather plays such an important part in mountain safety, a basic requirement is that you should always get a weather forecast before venturing onto the hill. There are various sources for these forecasts, some better than others.

Forecasts in newspapers vary greatly in quality. All suffer from the disadvantage that they cannot be updated on a regular basis. Some are simply reports of what the weather has been doing, whereas others forecast the likely changes. If there is an accompanying weather map, check whether it is a report map of the recent situation or a forecast map of the predicted situation. Somewhat better are forecasts on television and radio. These are often updated between bulletins to take account of unexpected changes. Some television forecasts, in particular, are extremely useful as the accompanying satellite pictures give a graphic representation of what is happening and what is approaching. The Sunday farming forecast which gives details of the week ahead is particularly useful.

National forecasts are useful in that they give a general overview of the situation. However, it is desirable to have a forecast that is a little more detailed. Local forecasts are available on local radio stations and by telephone, and there are often special forecasts for mountain walking in the more popular areas., These give details such as mountain and valley conditions, temperature inversions, lapse rates, freezing level, cloud base, precipitation, wind speed and direction at various heights, etc. Details are available through local telephone directories and are often publicised in outdoor magazines. Additionally, many of the better gear shops in popular areas have a weather board which is updated daily. If you have access to a fax, it is possible to get forecasts direct from the Meteorological Office. There is a range of forecasts available both national and local, some with accompanying maps or satellite pictures. For further details telephone the Meteorological Office helpline on 01344-854435.

## Self forecasts

Professional forecasting is a complex science, the weather is a fickle thing, and even the experts will acknowledge that they sometimes get it wrong! It therefore makes sense to have at least a basic working knowledge of frontal systems, airstreams, and the effects of topography. In this way you can modify the general picture to suit the local area, and can make some judgement of unexpected changes to the published forecast. In the same way that there are accident black-spots on the roads, there are also weather black-spots in the mountains, so it always pays to ask local advice. People who live and work in the mountains are in a far better position to know the idiosyncrasies of their local hills than are visitors.

When out on the hill, be observant. Take note of any changes in cloud type, wind direction and strength, and temperature. Try to build up an overall picture of what is happening. When looking at your map, think about the ways in which the local topography may affect the general weather, and never be afraid to turn back if you think the conditions warrant it or may do so within the near future.

# 8 Mountain environment

Famous Alpine guide Gaston Rébuffat maintained that there was more to being a mountaineer than learning how to climb. He believed that a good understanding of mountains and the environment was equally important, if not fundamental. The truth of this is easily demonstrated by the fact that, when out on the hill, you can always recognise experienced mountaineers by the way in which they appear to move effortlessly, no matter what the terrain. Less experienced parties tend to go through periods where they stumble and stagger and generally flounder around. As with so many of the skills of mountaincraft, learning to read the mountains and the terrain in order to choose a safe and suitable route is something which develops only after years of experience – you cannot expect to be proficient at route finding during early sojourns into the hills.

## Mixed ground

On the open fells there should be little difficulty in choosing a suitable route, but there will undoubtedly be times when you are faced with areas which contain a wide variety of features, from heather terraces through damp gullies to loose rock and small outcrops. The key to moving with the minimum difficulty through such terrain is to plan early, both through map interpretation and observation.

Try to work out a route which takes you along the lines of least resistance, and note the position of prominent features along the way which will help you keep to your chosen line. This can be difficult at first as things which look obvious from afar can often be far less obvious when you get closer. Do not forget, also, that you get a foreshortened viewpoint when looking at a slope from below, and an exaggerated viewpoint when looking down a slope. Particularly in conditions of low light, it can be extremely difficult to judge both depth and distance, and you will get a flattened perspective making it difficult to judge the best route.

When ascending through mixed ground where there is a profusion of outcrops, be aware of the increasing drop beneath you – it is very easy to scramble upwards gaining vast amounts of height without realising. In addition to route planning in broad terms, try to select a route in more detail as you go along. When descending, try to choose concave slopes *(see page 76)* which are as open as possible, and never jump down an outcrop. For one thing, it may be further than it seems; for another, you may not be able to climb back up the drop if you find your way on blocked. Always downclimb slowly and carefully – if you can descend in this way you should be able to re-ascend if necessary.

## Boulder fields and scree

The best boulder field is an avoided boulder field! However, it is sometimes necessary to cross them. The best approach is a deliberate one, but move carefully, choosing your route and concentrating on your foot placements.

Resist the temptation to leap from boulder to boulder, for not only can even the biggest of boulders move, but also the flat, inviting surface may be greasy. Be aware, too, that in certain areas, the edges of individual stones can be razor sharp. Take extra care where the boulders are overgrown with vegetation. Fronds of bracken and clumps of heather and bilberry can conceal gaps between the boulders which lie waiting to grab an unwary ankle.

Inclined boulder fields and scree slopes are potentially more hazardous, for if one boulder moves it is likely to set off a chain reaction *(see also page 97)*.

## Stonefall

Although it is not usually regarded as a major mountain hazard in Britain, stonefall does occur and people are injured by it each year. The three most common causes of stonefall are human action, freeze thaw action, and the effects of lightning. If scrambling, especially on big mountain cliffs, it would be prudent to wear a helmet.

When walking on or near a slope which contains loose boulders, be aware of other people. If there are people above you, work on the basis that they are idiots and take extra note when they are anywhere near vertically above you. If they are crossing above you, it may be wise to stop and watch until they are safely past so that if they do dislodge anything you get as much warning as possible.

Take great care, too, not to dislodge any rocks yourself, and if something starts to move, bellow "Below!" at the top of your voice. Do this even if you cannot see anyone below you – there may be someone hidden from view, and falling boulders can travel a surprising distance. Many people are unaware of the horizontal distance a falling boulder can travel – because it will glance off other rocks as it descends it is fair to say that a boulder can travel as far horizontally as it can vertically. Although the temptation can sometimes be almost irresistible, avoid trundling boulders deliberately.

Stonefall can also occur when there is no-one around to start it. This is usually due to freeze-thaw action in which water trapped in cracks in the rock freezes, expands, cracks the rock still further, and then melts. Freeze-thaw occurs most commonly in spring and autumn, and stonefall is most likely shortly after the sun has hit the crag. Where this is a common occurrence, there will be a build-up of loose boulders below the crag, the most obvious form being scree. If the scree is old and is only occasionally added to, it is known as dead scree and is recognisable by the fact that it has been colonised by vegetation. Active scree, on the other hand, has little if any vegetation which indicates that it is still being added to on a regular basis. If your route takes you up, down, or across scree, try to minimise the dangers *(see page 97).*

Freeze-thaw is not the only natural cause of stonefall. Heavy rain can wash away soil leaving rocks teetering on the brink; the vibrations from the noise of thunder can shake boulders free, lightning can literally shatter rock sending bits flying everywhere, and prolonged dry periods can cause the soil to shrink, freeing otherwise solid boulders. Therefore it makes sense to consider recent weather conditions when walking through areas where there is potential for stonefall.

Arguably the most dangerous areas for stonefall are gullies. No matter how well-used these are, they always contain loose material. Indeed, there are gullies which, once reasonably solid, are now becoming fraught with danger through the erosion caused by overuse. If you are caught in stonefall in a gully, there is very little you can do for the rocks will ricochet all over the place. If your route takes you into gullies, be aware of the different techniques you can use in an attempt to minimise the dangers *(see page 99)*.

## Bog

Bog is far more unpleasant than it is dangerous – indeed, the bottomless bog is more an old wives' tale than a reality. However, due to climate and poor drainage, many mountain areas contain large tracts of boggy land which are best avoided if possible. Admittedly, this can be difficult in areas such as Kinder Scout, Bleaklow, and parts of the Carmarthen Fan which appear to consist of little else.

If you must cross such areas, you may be able to keep out of the wettest areas by planning your route between patches of vegetation such as heather, heath and bilberry which do not like having their roots permanently waterlogged.

If you plan your route carefully you should never get into serious difficulties. However, if you find yourself sinking deeper and deeper into the mire, don't panic, for if you struggle, you will only sink deeper. Take off your rucksack, place it on the ground in front of you and lean forward, spreading your weight over as great an area as possible, then try to ease your legs out of the ooze.

If you cannot free yourself, rock backwards and forwards in order to create an air-space around your legs. If this does not work, try to form an air space by some other means (using you hands, tent poles, walking sticks, or anything else that comes to hand), then place your hands behind your thighs to give extra power to pull them out. If your companions have something to throw to you to give you some purchase, so much the better.

## Flood

Mention of river crossing techniques has already been made on *page 108*, but it may be useful for you to know a little about the mechanisms of flood. First and foremost, bear in mind that floods can occur even when you have not felt a drop of rain all day. For example, a localised rainstorm on a nearby hill can affect the state of a river many miles away. In winter conditions, you should also take into consideration the effects of the thaw. A sharp rise in temperature when the mountains are snowclad can have a significant effect on the level of streams in the area.

Mountain streams tend to rise and fall at an alarming

rate due partly to the nature of the terrain they drain, and partly to the fact the rainfall in mountain regions tends to be more intense than in the lowlands. In simplistic terms (with apologies to any hydrologists reading), when rain falls on the ground it drains into small trickles which merge into bigger rivulets which merge into small streams and so on.

At each merging, the amount of water flowing increases dramatically. Alongside this, the banks of the river create friction which effectively slows water down, so that in a flood situation, the water behind eventually begins to overtake the water in front. The end result is a sudden rise in water level known as a flood pulse which can carry surprising amounts of debris before it. Not only can it uproot plants from banks and snap up overhanging branches, it can also roll sizeable boulders along the river bed.

Mountaineers in general appear to have only scant regard for the power of moving water. If you wish to know more about this, ask an experienced canoeist to take you to a bridge across a mountain river and read the water for you.

## Ice

Ice can occur in many different forms in the mountains, from hard black ice, through brittle blue ice, to verglas, hoar and rime. All will have an effect on conditions underfoot. Of course, there does not have to be snow around for there to be ice. Any water on the mountain will obviously freeze if there is a sharp frost, and sheets of water ice are a common occurrence in certain areas, especially on damp paths and below spring lines. If this only occurs in patches, it may be possible to detour around it. Alternatively, if the sheet is only thin, it may be possible to stamp through the crust. The wisdom of such action can only be judged at the time. If there has been a heavy dew, or if it has rained before a drop in temperature, frozen turf can present serious difficulties. This can make onward progress extremely difficult, and upward progress extremely hazardous, especially if there are any drops nearby. Indeed, progress may only be safely possible wearing crampons.

One of the most likely ice conditions to cause problems is that of verglas. This is a clear, wafer-thin layer of ice which coats rocks, sometimes invisibly. It can be caused directly by the freezing of meltwater on rock surfaces, or indirectly as when raindrops freeze immediately on contact with sub-zero rock. It can also occur in patches – one minute you are walking on rough rock, the next you are skidding on an invisible sheet of ice. Crampons are ineffective on verglas as it is generally too thin to provide any purchase for the points.

Atmospheric icing occurs in a number of forms, the most common of which are rime ice and hoar frost. Rime ice is a soft deposit of ice which builds up on the windward sides rocks. It is formed from the water-droplets in clouds and, over a period, due to shifting wind directions, can build up into large, feathery flakes which totally cover rock pinnacles and flakes. It can also form on snow in which case it is known as graupel. Similar to rime deposits is hoar frost. This is a shimmering layer of fragile ice crystals formed by the crystallisation of water vapour direct onto freezing surfaces. If the vapour crystallises on lying snow it is known as surface hoar.

Ice is heavy, and broken ice can have razor sharp edges. In certain conditions you would therefore be wise to beware the danger of falling ice. This is particularly true after prolonged spells where the temperature hovers just below zero allowing a steady build up of water ice. Any thaw could precipitate the downfall of large quantities of ice, so be wary of walking below icy crags in such conditions. Bear in mind, too, the possibilities of stone fall *(see page 201)* and cornice collapse *(see below)*.

## Cornice

A cornice is basically a mass of unstable, over-hanging snow which is formed by wind action at the top of a slope. Although in its textbook form it is often shown as being severely overhanging, it can be less obvious and may simply appear as a false edge. Cornices occur due to a build up of snow on the leeward side of a ridge or scarp edge.

It is the angle of the windward slope which determines the size and shape of the cornice. If this slope is long, gentle and smooth, the cornice will be correspondingly large; conversely, if the windward slope is short, steep and uneven, the cornice will generally be far smaller *(see figure 42)*. Thus you are far more likely to find large cornices on the edge of a plateau than on a knife-edged ridge.

Cornices present a potential hazard both when

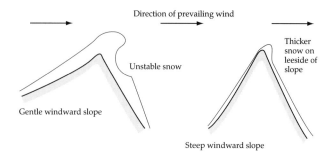

Unstable snow

Gentle windward slope

Thicker snow on leeside of slope

Steep windward slope

*Figure 42: cornice development and slope angle*

*Figure 43: cornice fracture line*

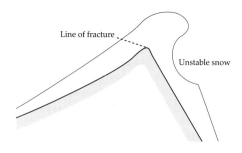

Line of fracture

Unstable snow

approached from above and below. When approaching from above, the most obvious danger is that of getting too close to the edge and falling through. However, the greater danger is that of

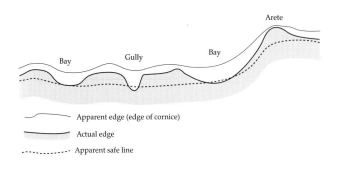

Apparent edge (edge of cornice)

Actual edge

Apparent safe line

*Figure 44: cornice hazards*

your weight causing a section of the cornice to collapse, for the fracture line is much further back from the edge than many people imagine *(see figure 43)*. Even if you realise this danger, there are situations in which an apparently safe route can take you inside the fracture line *(see figure 44)*. Good map interpretation is therefore of vital importance, and you should aim to gain a safe vantage point from which to view the edge whenever possible.

Particularly hazardous is searching for the start of a descent route. Sometimes the extent of the danger zone may be obvious from fracture lines, slumps and partial collapses; at other times it may be possible for you to gain a vantage point from which to judge the extent of the cornice. If you are unsure and must walk close to the edge in order to find the correct route, it would be prudent for you to rope up and be held on a belay. If there is no suitable natural anchor available, you will need to manufacture one with your ice axe. Such techniques are beyond the scope of this book for the reasons outlined earlier when discussing winter skills.

When approaching from below, or simply passing below a corniced slope, the most obvious danger is that of the cornice collapsing on top of you. There are a number of factors to consider. Firstly, the fact that a cornice is there at all is an indication of potential avalanche conditions *(see below)* for there is often a build-up of unstable snow on the slope beneath. Secondly, all cornices are inherently unstable and may collapse at any time. While physical examination from below is not recommended (!), a glance at neighbouring slopes for signs of recent debris may give clues as to the likelihood of imminent collapse. If a nearby cornice has collapsed, it is likely that there will be further collapses in the near future. However, do not be lulled into a false sense of security if no other cornices have collapsed, for the one above you may be the first to drop!

The weather conditions, both current and over the preceding few days, will also play a significant part in the stability of any cornice. Whilst it should be obvious that thaw conditions spell danger, recent heavy snowfall or winds strong enough to cause drifting will result in a build-up of snow which may, in itself, cause the cornice to collapse. As it happens, heavy snowfall and strong drifting are also classic avalanche conditions. This simply magnifies the potential danger for if an avalanche does not occur independently, under these circumstances a collapsing cornice is almost certain to trigger one.

# Avalanche

Over the past decade, much publicity has been given of the danger of avalanche, yet it is fair to say that a large number of hillwalkers still do not fully appreciate the risks. It is also fair to say that the mechanisms at work in avalanche are so complex that no-one fully understands them. Although this is an important safety consideration for anyone visiting the mountains under winter conditions, there is quite simply insufficient space here for me to do anything but give a brief overview of the main factors. Those wishing to know more will find details of relevant books in the bibliography.

We have already seen that different conditions will produce different types of snowflake. Thus the type of snow deposited in one snowfall may well be totally different to the type of snow deposited in the next. Additionally, the snow on the ground may well have undergone some changes before being covered by the new snow – for example, it may have been partially melted and have a crust on it or there may be surface hoar present. Over successive snowfalls one can therefore get a build up of several layers of snow, each with a different character. If two neighbouring layers of snow are of different hardness, or if layers are lubricated in some way (by a layer of unstable crystals or a sheet of water), a line of weakness is formed along which large masses of snow can slide.

A snowflake is inherently unstable and will change its shape as time goes by. There are three main processes at work in this situation. In destructive metamorphism (also known as equi-temperature metamorphism), the individual snowflakes become simplified, changing from angular crystals to rounded pellets. This initially results in a lack of cohesion between the individual particles, although eventually they will freeze together to form a layer. In practical terms, what happens is that the snow settles and then becomes more stable. This process happens most readily when the snowpack remains just below freezing. However, the colder the snowpack, the longer the process will take.

If the temperature oscillates around 0°C, the process of melt-freeze metamorphism occurs. During the day, when the temperature is above freezing, some of the crystals melt. When the temperature drops below freezing, the water so formed refreezes and bonds the crystals together. This process can result in a highly stable snow pack, but there are other considerations as well. For example, the water formed can percolate through the snowpack until its reaches an impermeable layer, such as could be caused by destructive metamorphism. When this happens it will flow along the boundary between this layer and the one above, effectively lubricating the joint.

Constructive metamorphism (or temperature gradient metamorphism) occurs when temperatures remain below freezing for a considerable period of time. When this happens there is a temperature gradient from the ground to the snow surface, and this allows water vapour to rise through the layers. If this continues for any length of time, it can result in the formation of large unstable crystals which, in addition to forming a lubricating layer, also represent a weakness which can fail suddenly and cause an avalanche.

One final type of metamorphism is found during sudden thaw. Under these conditions the crystalline structure of the snow can be destroyed before the snow melts, causing the whole snowpack to flow down the slope. This can be extremely dangerous as large quantities of debris are carried with the slide. A further problem is that the whole mass may freeze solid within only a few minutes of stopping.

Theory is all well and good, but we should be more concerned with practicalities. For a start, given the right conditions, avalanches can occur anywhere. Although they are most common in the Scottish hills, they also occur on a regular basis in places such as the Lake District and Snowdonia, and have been reported from the Brecon Beacons and even the South Downs! Avalanches will only occur if there is sufficient snow. The greater the amount of snow, the greater the risk of avalanche. 80% of all avalanches occur during or within 24hrs of heavy snowfall.

The angle of slope also plays an important part. Although it is commonly believed that the steeper the slope, the more likely the risk of avalanche, there comes a point where a slope is so steep that it will not allow large accumulations of snow and the risk therefore declines. The most dangerous slopes are those where large amounts of snow can build up. These are of medium angle, the highest risk being on slopes of between 30° and 45°, although there is a risk on any slope of between about 20° and 60°.

Moreover, the shape of slope will have an effect. All snow will slowly migrate down a slope due to the effects of gravity. If the slope if uniform, the process is usually a slow one. If the slope isconcave, there is compression of the layers at the point of concavity; however, if the slope is convex, an area of tension results and this can cause the layers of snow to fracture, and a significant number of avalanches start from such points. Another governing factor is the type of surface on which the snow pack lies. Slopes of long grass, mobile scree and smooth rock slabs provide little cohesion for the snow, and therefore the risk of avalanche from such slopes is increased.

One cannot assess the avalanche risk without taking past wind conditions into consideration. Not only will high winds cause large accumulations of snow through drifting, they will also deposit snow in layers of windslab. Generally speaking, the higher the windspeed, the harder the windslab. Successive windslabs may only be marginally attached to one another and therefore present a very high avalanche risk. Slab avalanches are the most commonly occurring type of avalanche in the British mountains. They are also the most difficult to predict. Do not underestimate their danger.

Although avalanches occur naturally, most of them involving people are caused by their victims. Before setting out on a winter expedition, ask local advice. Avoid the hills within 48hrs of heavy snowfall (or longer if it is particularly cold), and be wary of sudden changes in temperature, especially moving from cold conditions to mild conditions. If you think there may be a risk, keep to the high ground and avoid convex slopes and those between 30° and 45°.

Avoid gullies and narrow or enclosed valleys, and keep to windward slopes where possible. Look out for signs of recent or impending avalanche activity such as collapsing cornices, areas of subsidence, and cracks (especially when they run parallel to the slope), and take warning from small slides of slab when you move your feet.

You can also assess the risk by digging a snowpit using either a shovel or your ice axe. This should be dug in an area away from any risk of avalanche, but which is at about the same altitude and facing in the same direction as the suspect slope. The pit should be about 1 metre wide, and should ideally be dug down to ground level. The back wall should be smoothed so that there is a clear indication of any differences between snow layers. What you are looking for are large differences between hardness or water content in adjoining layers, and three tests should be carried out. Regarding hardness, it is usual to work on a scale of 1 to 5, 1 being soft powder snow and 5 being hard, consolidated snow-ice.

If any adjacent layers have a difference in hardness of 3 or more, there is a high avalanche risk. With regard to water content, work on a scale of 1 to 5 again, 1 being dry powder which will not stick together, and 5 being wet snow which releases water when squeezed. Again, any large differences should be taken as warning signs, with the added proviso that the water in wet layers (4 or 5) can act as a lubricant and increase the chances of avalanche.

Finally, look at the basic structure of the snow. Particularly dangerous are large cup-shaped crystals and rounded grains of graupel, both of which can form an ideal sliding surface. Once you have completed these observations, use the shaft of your axe to cut two vertical slots just under a metre apart in the back wall of your pit. Now get a companion to approach slowly from above, so that his weight causes the snow to slump. If a slab breaks away cleanly between two layers, this represents weak bonding and the ease with which it breaks indicates the ease with which an avalanche could occur.

If you find yourself in a situation where it is imperative that you cross a slope which you consider to be suspect, do so one at a time, choosing if possible the shortest route between two stable points such as trees or outcrops. Before starting to cross, loosen your rucksack, raise your hood and zip up your jacket to give some protection to your face, and remove any ice-axe loop. When crossing, move slowly and steadily, heading slightly downhill.

If the slope does avalanche there is probably very little that you will be able to do. If you are on the edge of the slide, you may be able to escape, but if not you should try to stay where you are for as long as possible – the longer you stay still, the less material there will be to bury you. Try to keep upright with your back to the snow. If you start to move, get rid of your ice axe and rucksack, cover your face, keep your mouth closed and try to roll towards the nearest edge of the slide. The critical period for survival is as the avalanche slows. If you are still conscious struggle with all your might to make as large an airspace around you as you can and claw your way towards any light before the snow sets solid.

Eighty percent of avalanche fatalities are caused by suffocation, so keep your eyes on your companions as they cross a suspect slope, and try to track their position if they are engulfed. If they are buried, try to note the position at which they were caught and the position at which they were last seen, as this may give an indication of where they are. Speed is of the essence. As soon as the slope has stabilised, do an immediate surface search and dig in any likely places.

If you visit the hills in winter, it would be wise to consider carrying an avalanche beacon or, at the very least, an avalanche cord. Avalanche cords are long lengths of brightly coloured nylon which have arrows pointing in one direction along their length. You tie the end towards which the arrows point around your waist and leave the rest trailing when you cross a suspect slope.

If you are avalanched, some part of the cord may rest on the surface and this will guide rescuers to your position fairly quickly. Avalanche beacons, on the other hand, are far more expensive, but they may save a life. These are simple radio transceivers which can be set either to transmit or receive. These should be carried on your person and not in your rucksack for you may be parted from your rucksack if you are avalanched. Under normal circumstances you should switch the beacon to transmit mode.

When searching for an overwhelmed person, you set them to receive mode. Different models work in different ways, but most work on the principle that increasing signal strength indicates decreasing distance from the casualty. Different models also work on different frequencies, so it makes sense to check that all beacons in the same party work on the same frequency.

## Whiteout

Mention has already been made of whiteout conditions on *page 188*. If you are caught in such conditions, accurate navigation becomes imperative, especially if you are in areas where there are drops and possible cornices. It is no exaggeration to say that you could be standing on the edge of a crag and not even know it is there! You will be disorientated, you will probably stumble and fall over a fair amount, and you will need to concentrate on what you are doing. Because you have no horizon, your judgement of distance and time will be impaired, so use Naismith's Rule and pacing. Compass navigation will necessitate a leap-frogging technique.

# 9 Ailments

I have strong views about First Aid training: I feel it should be a compulsory subject at both primary and secondary levels of education. Be that as it may, when you consider how far you might be from front-line medical assistance when you are in the mountains, it makes sound sense for every visitor to the hills to have at least a working knowledge of basic first aid techniques. I would therefore encourage you to get some training, preferably on a course aimed specifically at outdoor first aid. Although it is not possible for me to go into a great amount of detail, no book about mountain safety would be complete without at least a passing mention of some of the more common ailments.

## Mountain hypothermia

Of all the ailments met in the mountains, it is mountain hypothermia, or exhaustion-exposure, which is the most insidious. Despite the fact that it is easily avoidable in the vast majority of situations, it is responsible for a large number of deaths each year. One of the main reasons for this may be that, notwithstanding continual efforts by organisations such as the British Mountaineering Council, the condition is still largely misunderstood by many hillgoers. To give a classic example, most people associate mountain hypothermia with the cold, but the colder it is, the warmer you dress, and the more aware of the temperature you are. The sad fact of the matter is that mountain hypothermia most commonly occurs when the ambient temperature is between 5°C and 10°C.

When discussing the layer system *(page 20)*, I described the body as a machine with two main parts: the core (containing all the vital organs), and the shell (the skin, flesh and bones). It was stated that this human machine had a set of ideal operating conditions, the most important of which was the temperature of the core. Hypothermia occurs when the temperature of the core drops below its optimum value of 37°C, the immediate result being a marked decrease in the efficiency of the vital organs.

The brain (and thus the personality) is one of the first things to be affected, so different individuals will react in different ways. Because of this, although there are several parallels, no two cases of mountain hypothermia have ever been exactly the same. The most straightforward approach is to work on the basis that, in marginal conditions, any change of character or unusual behaviour should be regarded as indicative of possible hypothermia.

Several other factors will have an effect. Firstly, the word exhaustion is important here, because the body requires energy in order to produce heat. This is one of the reasons that a good, cooked breakfast and frequent high energy snacks are vital in poor conditions. Secondly, even on good days, people who have suffered an accident and have gone into shock are at greater risk from the condition, and should therefore have their heat loss minimised as a matter of urgency. Thirdly, psychology appears to play a vital role and the will to live is essential. Finally, always treat the condition as serious and provide treatment with the utmost urgency. It is not overly melodramatic to say that the time between onset and death can be less than two hours.

To treat mountain hypothermia effectively, you must know a little more about cause and effect. The body normally maintains its core temperature to within very fine limits, balancing heat losses and gains through a variety of mechanisms. In terms of hypothermia, it is the way in which the capillaries below the surface of the skin react which is most important. If heat gain exceeds heat loss, these capillaries open up through the mechanism of vasodilation. This allows more blood to pass close to the surface of the skin so that heat can be shed. This is accompanied by sweating in order that evaporation can increase the amount of heat lost.

If, on the other hand, heat loss exceeds heat gain, the capillaries close down through the mechanism of vasoconstriction. This reduces the amount of blood flowing to the shell and therefore reduces the amount of heat loss at the core. Additionally, because muscular activity produces heat, we start to shiver as a means of creating more heat. The reason your fingers feel numb and you fumble when you are cold is because vasoconstriction has reduced the blood flow to the muscles and reduced their efficiency.

It is when the heat loss continues that we enter the problem area. As mentioned above, everyone reacts in a slightly different way. Although we can identify a number of phases, the signs and symptoms may overlap or may even be absent in certain individuals, so the following is a guide to what you may see.

The first phase – mild hypothermia – begins as the core temperature drops below 37°C. Coldness and fatigue are obvious common symptoms, and many sufferers experience cramp as vasoconstriction begins to reduce the blood supply to the muscles. As the core temperature decreases past 36°C, vasoconstriction will increase to the extent that the muscles start to become seriously affected, and sufferers will stumble, fumble, and display a general lack of co-ordination. Shivering becomes uncontrollable, and the skin may take on a pallid appearance. The efficiency of the brain, too, will start to deteriorate, and sufferers may become lethargic, apathetic, and withdrawn. At this stage, further deterioration can often be prevented simply by reducing heat loss. Beyond this stage, however, the situation becomes far more serious.

As the core temperature drops below 35°C, we enter the stage of moderate hypothermia. The situation has now become very serious indeed, and the most insidious aspects of the condition will begin to take affect. The brain will, by now, have become so affected that the sufferer may refuse to acknowledge that there is a problem, and may become abusive and even violent if you try help. As the body tries even harder to prevent further heat loss, vasoconstriction will increase to the extent that shivering will cease.

Muscular movement will become sluggish and erratic,

stumbling and pallor will increase, and it will take a long time for the sufferer to recover after increasingly frequent falls. At about 33°C, the vital organs will deteriorate rapidly, the most marked effects being on the brain and the visual cortex. Irrational behaviour (many people start taking off their clothes) and incoherence together with hallucination and other forms of visual disturbance are commonly reported, and many victims start suffering from amnesia. Make no mistake about it: people suffering from moderate hypothermia are very ill. Damage to the vital organs will be such that prevention of further heat loss will be insufficient to promote recovery, and the sufferer will have to be actively rewarmed.

As the core temperature drops below about 31°C, the sufferer enters the stage of severe hypothermia – a critical condition in which both heartbeat and respiration will begin to weaken. Stupor becomes increasingly apparent, and the pupils may begin to dilate. Below about 30°C, the heartbeat will become weak and irregular, and the sufferer will drift towards unconsciousness. Even if the heat loss is stopped immediately, death will occur within a matter of a few hours unless medical help is available. Indeed, by this stage, chemical changes will have taken place within the body which can lead to fatal complications on rewarming, so it is imperative that anyone who reaches this stage gets expert medical help as a matter of extreme urgency.

When the core temperature drops below 29°C we reach the stage of acute hypothermia in which most reflexes cease to function. Heartbeat and respiration will continue to weaken and become increasingly erratic. Below 28°C the autonomic nervous system governing heart beat and breathing will start to fail, and the sufferer may exhibit no noticeable pulse or breathing. However, it is imperative that you do not take the absence of breathing or pulse to indicate death. Extremely low core temperatures reduce the body's need for oxygen, and there are documented cases in which acutely hypothermic people have made a full recovery after having exhibited neither pulse nor respiration for over an hour.

The most common mistake after having diagnosed the onset of the condition is to head urgently for the nearest habitation, forcing the sufferer along. Unless this is at the earliest stages of mild hypothermia and habitation is very close (under an easy kilometre), this is totally the wrong thing to do, for any additional expenditure of energy by the sufferer can cause the core temperature to plummet with possibly fatal results.

In the most basic of terms, treatment is simple. No matter where you are, the most important thing to do is to stop any further heat loss, and the simplest way to do this is to find some sort of shelter from the wind, even if you have to make this yourself. This is where your cheap plastic survival bag can literally become a life saver.

Once in shelter, replace the sufferer's wet clothes with dry ones *(but see below)*, and place him in a survival bag which has been insulated from the ground with a sleepmat, rucksack, clothing, or anything else which comes to hand. You should now attempt active rewarming, the easiest way being to get someone to join the sufferer in the survival bag. If you can also give hot drinks and some high energy foods (your survival rations), so much the better.

A sleeping bag would also be useful, but make sure that someone else has warmed it first as the sufferer's shell temperature will be so low that he will be unable to warm a sleeping bag himself. Rewarming should be gentle and general – on no account should you attempt massage or vigorous rubbing, nor should you place warm objects against the sufferer's skin. Doing so would reverse the effects of vasodilation, causing the local capillaries to open allowing warm core blood to be replaced with cold shell blood. Giving alcohol to a hypothermic person will have the same effect.

Do not forget, that psychology plays a part in the treatment of any ailment. Give plenty of TLC (tender loving care) and calm reassurance no matter how worried you are. Think also of yourself and other members of the party: if conditions are such that one person is suffering, chances are others may be at risk especially if they are hanging around doing nothing.

Recovery from mild hypothermia can be rapid and may appear to be total. Even if this occurs, there should be no question of pushing on, as the sufferer will have been severely weakened by the condition. You must get him off the hill by the easiest and most sheltered route – this will not necessarily be the quickest. If recovery does not occur within two hours, or if the condition worsens, you should work on the basis that the moderate hypothermic stage has been reached and any further heat loss could prove fatal.

Although the treatment continues to be the same, there are now other factors to consider. For example, if on initial diagnosis you suspect the sufferer has already reached this stage, you will have to think carefully before removing any wet clothing, for this will contain a small amount of heat and provide a small amount of insulation. Removing wet clothing may result in an overall heat loss, and this must be avoided at all costs. Far better to place the sufferer in a survival bag, wet clothes and all, and then provide additional insulation over the top of the wet clothing. Additionally, no matter what the situation, moderate hypothermic casualties should always be regarded as stretcher cases, and a mountain rescue team should be called. Self-help is not advised.

Recovery from moderate hypothermia will not occur without the application of some form of external heat. If the sufferer is conscious, by all means administer hot sweet drinks and high energy foods. If you are carrying a tent, pitch it and place the sufferer inside together with as many of the party as comfortably possible. Also extremely useful in this situation are KISU's *(see page 249)*.

If the sufferer reaches the severe or acutely hypothermic phase, the situation has become extremely grave indeed. No matter what action is taken to reverse the heat loss, death is inevitable within a few hours unless specialist medical help is available. Summoning a mountain rescue team therefore becomes a matter of extreme urgency. All you can do on site is provide shelter, prevent any further heat loss, and provide general rewarming.

Finally, two points are worth reiterating. Firstly, assuming you know the sufferer reasonably well, the occurrence of any uncharacteristic behaviour in marginal conditions should be regarded as being indicative of exhaustion-exposure. Your usually mild-mannered companion may, for example, start to swear and curse and become belligerent. Secondly, assuming that you are not suffering, you are in a far better position to judge the condition of the sufferer than he is himself. Despite any denials on his part, it is essential that treatment begins as early as possible.

In 99% of cases, mountain hypothermia is totally avoidable. If you wear correct clothing and are neither over-ambitious nor foolhardy, it should never occur.

## Heat stroke

Going back to our analogy of the human machine, in the same way as a drop in core temperature will lead to serious problems, so too will a rise in core temperature. If you think of mountain hypothermia lying at one end of the temperature scale, heat stroke lies at the other. Indeed, whilst there are many similarities between the symptoms of the two conditions, the treatments are at opposite extremes.

When visiting the mountains in hot weather, and particularly in humid conditions, the heat gained through muscular exertion can be so intense that the body is unable to maintain its heat balance. The response to overheating is vasodilation accompanied by sweating. As the amount of overheating increases, so the amount of sweat produced increases. Even if this reduces the overheating, the loss of the fluid and the salts contained in the sweat can result in several problems, most noticeably heat cramp, which can be regarded as the first stage of heat stroke.

Heat cramp usually affects the stomach and leg muscles, and is excruciatingly painful. Not only are the effects exacerbated by vasodilation, but the increased blood flow to the shell may cause a decreased blood flow to the brain resulting in a general feeling of weakness, dizziness and possibly fainting. The condition should be taken seriously as it is a warning sign that heat stroke is a distinct possibility, and treatment should be immediate. The sufferer should be put in some form of shade and allowed to rest. If there is no natural shade available you must create some with a survival bag or something similar. Cramped muscles should be eased by stretching and massaging the affected areas. It is also essential that the sufferer is given plenty to drink. Because of the salt loss, the ideal liquid is some form of electrolyte replacement drink, but water to which salt has been added at the rate of a couple of pinches per litre is just as effective (and far cheaper). Do not add more salt than this as at greater concentrations the liquid becomes emetic!

Prompt action will almost always result in rapid recovery. However, as with hypothermia, there should be no question of continuing as the sufferer will have been severely weakened by the experience. He should be led slowly off the hill by the easiest and most shaded route, and allowed frequent rests and drinks.

If heat cramp is ignored, or the level of sweating is

not reduced, there will be a real danger of dehydration. Further physical exertion could cause the core temperature to rise, and the inevitable result is heat exhaustion, a far more serious condition. The symptoms are in many ways an extension of those of heat cramp: the sufferer will complain of nausea and headache, will feel fatigued and light headed, and may vomit or faint. Pulse and respiration rates may increase as more and more blood is pumped to the shell but, somewhat paradoxically, the skin may feel cold and clammy. Again, some form of shade is of the utmost importance, but now the essential liquid should only be given in sips as the sufferer may not be able to keep it down.

Moreover, it is important actively to assist the body to lose heat, and this is best done by loosening or even removing clothing, fanning, and applying wet clothes to the skin and particularly to the forehead. Given shade, active cooling and liquid, recovery will usually occur given time, and this will be assisted by giving more frequent drinks once the nausea has dissipated. Even when the sufferer appears to have recovered, it is important that he be given plenty of time to rest before being led slowly homewards by the easiest and coolest route, for not only can heat exhaustion recur with frightening ease, but it is also only a small step away from heat stroke. Heat stroke is an extremely serious condition and anyone suffering from it will be critically ill. In this final stage the core temperature has increased to such an extent that the vital functions start to deteriorate. Unfortunately, one of the first things to malfunction is the mechanism of vasodilation which results in the body being unable to lose heat. Consequently, the core temperature will rise rapidly and death will result within a very short period of time.

As victims of heat stroke are suffering from a breakdown in their vital organs, they often display many of the symptoms of mountain hypothermia, particularly those of irrational behaviour, aggression and abuse, in addition to most of the symptoms of heat exhaustion. Somewhat confusingly, the skin may either be red, hot and dry or cool, pale and damp. The core temperature could well be as high as 41°C, and immediate and active cooling is imperative for otherwise the sufferer will go into convulsions and die.

It will not be sufficient simply to put the sufferer in shade; you must remove clothing, apply wet clothes or, if available, cool water to the forehead and the back of the neck, and fan him vigorously. Only give liquid if he is conscious, and then only in sips. Heat stroke victims are critically ill and should always be regarded as stretcher cases, even on the very rare occasions that they appear to make a total recovery. Medical advice should be sought in all cases.

As with hypothermia, the condition is avoidable. On particularly hot days avoid strenuous walking, particularly around noon, and drink far more liquid than you feel you need, a little at a time but often. If you eat a balanced diet you should not need salt tablets, but some people, particularly those who sweat profusely, will find them useful. They should be taken in the morning as a precautionary measure rather than being used as first-aid items on the hill.

Many people suffer from mild dehydration on the

hills, relying on traditional evening social sessions to get them out of water debt! Whilst mild, short term water debt will not cause too many problems, it is not good practice, and you should always take plenty to drink and sip little but often in order to maintain a good fluid balance.

## Frostbite

Like heat stroke, frostbite can be regarded as a progressive condition ranging from frostnip (a far more common condition than generally realised), through superficial frostbite (a common occurrence in emergency situations), and finally to deep frostbite (rare in the British mountains). It is caused initially by a reduction in blood flow to the extremities such as occurs in vasoconstriction or if you wear clothing or footwear which is too tight. As the warm blood flow is reduced, so the surrounding flesh begins to cool, and if the air temperature is low enough and there is insufficient protection, ice crystals will being to grow between the cells and the tissue will literally freeze.

The first stage of the condition, in which the tissue has just started to freeze, is frostnip. Most commonly affected are the toes, fingers, ears, nose and cheeks, so if you are out in particularly cold conditions and any of these areas begins to feel warm or numb after having been painfully cold, you should suspect frostnip and investigate further. Frostnip is easily detectable as the affected part will be numb and white. Treatment is simple and effective – you should rewarm the afflicted part. Do not rub the area, however, as this could cause more damage. Cheeks, ears and nose can be warmed with the hands, and fingers can be placed under the armpits, preferably beneath a couple of layers of clothing. Rewarming toes is somewhat more problematic and generally requires outside help from someone who is a true friend! The best results are gained by removing socks and placing your feet under their jacket, preferably on their stomach, under their armpits, or in their crutch. Recovery is usually fairly rapid, but it may be accompanied by stinging pins-and-needles sensations, and is often painful. The damage caused to the tissue will also result in increased susceptibility in the future, so prevention is far better than cure. If you cannot get the feeling back to the area within about an hour, you should treat the condition as frostbite.

If you think you may have frostnip, particularly frostnipped feet, it is important that you stop, investigate, and take appropriate action even if the removal of gaiters, boots and socks seems like a lot of bother. If you press on regardless and ignore the warning signs you could do yourself some lasting damage, for if the freezing is allowed to continue, superficial frostbite is inevitable. This is far more serious as the cells now freeze, rupture and start to die. In addition to being numb, the skin will have the appearance and possibly the texture of white candle wax, and small blisters may form.

The immediate treatment is the same as that for frostnip – the affected part should be rewarmed. On no account should you rub the affected area, especially not with snow (a common misconception). Doing so is a bad mistake on three counts: firstly, you could rupture the cells which are already damaged, secondly, snow crystals act as an abrasive on the damaged skin, and thirdly, the resultant moisture evaporates leading to further cooling. Recovery from frostbite is not so easy as from frostnip, and if feeling has not returned within about half an hour, there is little else you can do without medical help. In this situation you should get off the hill with the part still frozen. If you do succeed in regaining colour and feeling to the affected area, you must make every effort to ensure that it does not re-freeze as you retreat as this will cause greatly increased damage. In all cases, even when recovery appears to have taken place, appropriate medical advice should be sought as soon as possible for there may be lasting damage to tissue and nerves.

Like so many of these conditions, both frostnip and frostbite are avoidable in the vast majority of cases. If you are clothed correctly and discipline yourself to stop and check if you suspect the onset of the condition, there should be no problem. It is particularly important that you avoid wearing any clothing or footwear which restricts movement or circulation. Wet socks and mittens will increase the effects of wind-chill, and can result in frostbite when the temperature is only just below freezing. Over-mitts and gaiters are essential in winter. On a more positive note, constant fiddling, wriggling your fingers and toes, will result in a small amount of muscular heat and better circulation.

Finally, when camping in winter, be careful not to spill stove fuel (which freezes below 0°C) on bare hands, and avoid contact between flesh and bare metal.

## Snow blindness

Snow blindness is a very painful condition caused by overexposure to ultra-violet radiation. Although there can be similar effects after a long day on the hill in bright sunshine, the condition is mainly associated with sunlight reflecting off snow so that the UV radiation hits the eyes from below. The condition is even more likely on cloudy days as the cloudbase will itself reflect UV back down again! A major problem is that the damage is done before the symptoms make themselves felt.

Symptoms start with itching, dryness and irritation of the eyeball which quickly develops to the stage where it feels as if there is broken glass under the eyelid. Blinking becomes excruciatingly painful and in severe cases the eyelids may swell. Tear production often increases to the extent that the eyes water permanently. The condition is temporary and will go away of its own accord, given two or three days. During this time, the best relief is gained by lying quietly in a darkened room with cold compresses on the eyes. Analgesic may be taken to reduce the pain, but anaesthetic eye drops should be avoided as they tend to increase the recovery time. Avoid rubbing the eyes.

Prevention is better than cure, and is simply done by wearing good sunglasses or goggles. These should have lenses which filter harmful rays and are sufficiently tinted to reduce all glare. If glasses are worn, they should be close fitting and have some form of side baffle to prevent unfiltered light from entering. If you are caught in snowy conditions without suitable protection, or if you lose your glasses, you can get temporary protection by cutting a narrow horizontal slit in the cardboard cover of a map. This can be used to cover the eyes, held in place either with a spare bootlace, or by a jacket hood.

## Sunburn

No matter how much of a sun-worshipper you are, nor how well you tan, sunburn is potentially a serious problem in the mountains. The air is generally much clearer than in valley areas and this leads to greater amounts of UV radiation. The situation is particularly hazardous in winter when snow reflects the radiation upwards. Avoidance is easy through regular application of sun-screen with a filter factor of at least 8. Higher values are necessary for people with fair skins, and a total sunblock is advisable for sensitive skin. It should be applied to all exposed skin, and in winter conditions you should ensure that you apply it to the underside of your chin, the base of the earlobes and the nostrils. It is better to carry sunscreen in a pocket rather than in your rucksack as this encourages regular application. Lips should be protected with a high-filter lip salve.

## Blisters

Blisters are probably the most common complaint suffered by walkers, and their seriousness should not be underestimated. Although they usually cause nothing more than discomfort, they can be debilitating and can slow you down sufficiently to increase the possibility of benightment. If treated badly (or left untreated), they can also lead to serious problems if you are camping in the wild. A blister is simply the result of friction, the most common causes being badly fitting boots, ill-fitting socks, sensitive feet, or foreign bodies. Avoidance is simple – before the blister forms you will feel a hot-spot or soreness. You should discipline yourself to stop immediately this occurs and pad the area with zinc oxide plaster or a proprietary blister pad. If you continue until the blister is allowed to form, you should treat it by bursting it with a sterile needle, draining the fluid, and then covering it with a pad. Do not remove the blistered skin. Particularly effective are pads made from artificial skin – a special gel layer which provides not only padding, but also has antiseptic and lubricating qualities. Alternatively use a dressing held in place with zinc oxide plaster. If the blister has formed on a toe, the most effective way to pad it is by using micropore or tubular bandage. If the blister is particularly large, you should cut the plaster in such a way that it does not crease when applied. Once you arrive home (or at your campsite), remove the dressing, wash your feet to reduce the chance of infection, and let the blister breathe. If you are visiting the hills within the next few days, cover the affected area with artificial skin.

## More serious injuries

Everyone who visits the mountains should have a working knowledge of the ABC of first aid, for if something happens it could be some time before qualified medical help arrives. At the very least you should know the recovery position, how to give CPR, what to do in cases of severe bleeding, and how to deal with fractures.

# 10 Emergency procedures

Accidents can happen to anyone, no matter how experienced or well equipped. It therefore makes sense to have thought a little about what you would do in the event of an accident. The problem is that no two accidents are ever the same. There are so many variables (weather, location, terrain, people, nature of injury, time of day, equipment available, etc.) that every accident is unique. There are thus few, if any, hard and fast rules governing what you should do.

Having said this, there are certain areas where we can draw definite conclusions. For example, if you are the leader of a party, the order of your priorities is clear. Your first priority is to the rest of your party – it is pointless going to someone's aid if this results in further casualties. Your second priority is to yourself – it is of little use trying to help someone if you end up injured yourself. As cynical as it may sound, the casualty comes third. If you are a member of a party, the order still applies, for you should keep your eyes on your colleagues who may well be unable to cope with the situation as well as you. This is particularly important in marginal weather conditions when hypothermia is an ever-present risk for all members of the group in any emergency situation.

Similarly, you should try to stay cool, calm and

collected at all times. Granted, it is easy for me to write this sitting comfortably in front of a word processor whereas it is a totally different proposition when clinging to a heather ledge above an awesome drop in a howling gale. In any case, no-one knows how they will react to an emergency until it actually happens, but whatever the situation, you will not help matters by panicking. If you feel yourself losing control, try to focus your attention and "centre" yourself (to use the modern phrase). Calm yourself by consciously controlling your breathing, drawing in deep breaths and releasing them slowly.

## Rescue call-out procedures

Self-evacuation is never an easy option. Whilst there are certain things you can do to help yourself and the casualty, you should never delay in calling for help for fear of embarrassment or recrimination. The situation will be far worse if you try to do it all yourself and fail. In the most general of terms, you would be wise to summon assistance in all situations except those where the casualty is reasonably mobile, where the injuries are superficial, or where the journey off the hill is exceptionally short. Most mountain rescue teams would rather arrive to a situation which is less serious than was reported than be called out later to pick up a corpse.

Having said this, there have been a number of situations over the past few months where people with mobile phones have called mountain rescue when in all honesty, their situation was not that serious. Whilst a mobile phone can have obvious advantages in a real emergency, it should not be seen as an easy way out of trouble. Your initial call for help will probably be to people who may be nearby, and this is best done by giving the alpine distress signal. This consists of six good blasts on a whistle followed by a minute's silence, repeated as necessary. You should continue giving the signal until you are in visual contact with people coming to your aid. If you hear this signal, you should acknowledge the fact by giving the reply – three good blasts on a whistle followed by a minute's silence, repeated as necessary. Once again, you should repeat this acknowledgement until you are within visual contact with the distressed party. As it happens, any whistling in the mountains may be construed as being a distress signal, so never blow your whistle unless in distress or answering a distress call. If for some reason you have no whistle, the same signal can be given by shouting or waving a bright object such as a white handkerchief, orange survival bag or similar.

At night, flashing a torch (in conjunction with blasts on a whistle, if possible) could be useful. Having said all this there are two points worth bearing in mind. Firstly, if you are in distress it may well be that the weather conditions are so bad in terms of visibility and wind, that people only a couple of hundred metres away may not hear or see you. Secondly, whistles have been abused to such an extent that many people may well ignore anything but a clear alpine distress call or SOS (three quick blasts/flashes/waves followed by three long blasts/flashes/waves followed by a further three quick blasts/flashes/waves then a short pause before repeating the sequence all over again).

It is a great tradition of the mountains that the mountaineer looks after his own. If you suspect that a party may be in distress, try to investigate further. If you can reach them easily and safely, all well and good, but on no account should you jeopardise your own safety or that of your companions. If you hear a distress signal but for some reason cannot find out any more, give the acknowledgement a few times, then make your way quickly but safely to the nearest telephone or rescue post and notify mountain rescue. You will almost always be asked to stay by the telephone and await either further instructions or the arrival of a team member. This is because face-to-face discussions are invariably more informative than telephone conversations.

The call-out procedure for mountain rescue is simple. Either visit a manned post or (more likely) get to a telephone, dial 999, ask for the police then ask for mountain rescue. In order to proceed promptly and efficiently with the rescue, the team will need a lot of information. In particular, they will need to know the precise location of the incident. Although this is best done by giving a six figure grid reference, there may be times when this is not possible (when, for example, you have heard a distress signal but have been unable to investigate).

In such cases, give as much information as you can, by giving your position when you heard the distress signal, the direction from which it came, etc. If the incident has taken place on a rock climb, you should give the name of the crag, the name of the climb and the pitch on which the accident happened. Similar information should be given if the accident occurred on a scramble. Ideally, the rescue team should be able to go straight to the incident site from your description, and should know whether to approach from the top or bottom of a climb or scramble.

In addition to the location, the team will want to know such things as the time the accident occurred, the number of people injured and the nature of their injuries, the weather conditions at the incident site, the number of people remaining at the site, etc. Whether you are a member of the party or someone who has gone to their aid or is reporting their distress, many of the questions asked may seem irrelevant at the time. However, all these questions will be asked for good reasons.

## Self-help

It may sound trite, but the best way you can help yourselves is not to let the accident occur in the first place! Although unforseeable accidents do occur, the majority are avoidable. A good philosophy for mountain activities is "Bottle out and run away, live to climb another day!". Unfortunately, it often takes more courage to turn back than to push on regardless, especially if you have been planning the weekend away for some time.

Do not take unnecessary risks; if the weather looks threatening or something is going wrong, either turn back or modify your plans accordingly. After all, the mountain will always be there – there will always be another opportunity – and you will probably enjoy the experience all the more if you wait until the circumstances are more favourable.

If an accident does occur, try to stay cool, calm and collected, make sure that there is no risk to yourself or other members of the party, then go to the aid of the casualty. Administer immediate first aid as necessary, checking bleeding, breathing and heartbeat. If the casualty is unconscious, move him into the recovery position unless you suspect neck or spinal injury, in which case you should not move him unless not doing so will seriously prejudice his chances of survival. If the casualty is conscious, give him plenty of reassurance and TLC.

Do not underestimate the effects of medical shock, and always work on the basis that an injured person is far more likely to succumb to hypothermia. If you are able to move him, get him to a sheltered position, the most important consideration being protection from the wind. If you cannot move him, it may be necessary to build some form of shelter around him (see below). Give him extra warm clothing (dressing him yourself if necessary), and place him in a survival bag. Do not forget to insulate him from the ground. Reassure him at regular intervals.

Now is the time to use your emergency rations. If you can also provide a hot drink (either from a flask or, if you have the equipment, by starting a brew), so much the better. Hot, sweet drinks are of enormous benefit in cases of hypothermia and shock, and are a good morale booster for the remaining members of the party. Never try to give food or drink to an unconscious casualty or to anyone suffering from head, chest or abdominal injuries.

If you are alone with the casualty, you will have to make an extremely difficult decision – whether to stay with him, signal your distress and hope that help will soon arrive, or whether to leave him alone whilst you go and summon help yourself. There are no easy answers here – the decision can only be made at the time and will depend upon such things as location, nature of injuries, weather conditions, time of day, etc. If you decide to go and he is conscious, make sure he is as warm and as comfortable as possible. Reassure him once again, leave him your spare clothing plus a flask and emergency rations if possible, and make sure he has a whistle and a torch so that he can signal to any approaching rescue team. If you are carrying one, leave him a stove and pan so that he can make a hot drink himself. It may be several long hours before a rescue party arrives.

If he is unconscious, do all of the above and, if possible, tie him to an anchor so that if he regains consciousness he cannot wander off in a daze. This is important in the event of an accident on a rock climb or scramble, or if there is steep, rocky ground in the near vicinity. It is also a good idea to leave a reassuring note explaining what you are doing.

Before you leave, mark the precise position as prominently as you can using bright objects as markers. If you have a climbing rope, run it out in a line across the hillside so that there is a good chance of finding the position again, even in bad visibility. Once you have done as much as you can, make your way carefully to the nearest telephone by the easiest route, always remembering that his safety now relies on your safety. Never take unnecessary risks.

If you are a member of a larger party, you must decide how many people should go for help and how many people should stay with the casualty. Again, there are a number of considerations, the most important one being that, wherever possible, at least two people should go for help. If the weather conditions are marginal, anyone who stays is at risk from hypothermia, so it may at first glance appear that as few people should stay as possible. However, the other side of the coin is that the more people there are in a shelter, the warmer it will be, and this will not only reduce the risk of hypothermia but will also help a conscious casualty.

There are never any easy decisions in a mountain emergency. All you can do is think about the effects of the weather, the surroundings and the situation both on the casualty and on the remainder of the party. In the heat of the moment, do not neglect to think about the effect on yourself.

## Improvised shelters

Even where there has not been an accident, you may have made an error of judgement and still be left high on the hill in gathering darkness. Indeed, benightment is an especially high risk in winter when mountain days are short, and you would do well to think about finding shelter earlier rather than later, for trying to build a shelter in unknown terrain in the dark can be a nightmare. Having said this, try to get as far down the mountain as you can, but once benightment is inevitable, stop as soon as you see anything which can be used to provide shelter.

In some areas it is possible to find superb natural shelters formed by overhanging boulders or piles of huge rocks. If there is natural shelter, use it. However, the chances of you coming across one of these by accident at the precise time you need it are slim. Even if there is natural shelter, you may well be able to improve it. In any case, some form of shared activity can be a great morale booster. Having people hanging around doing nothing is not going to help matters, and could well precipitate further problems.

Getting people involved and doing something will not only take their minds off the blacker side of the situation, but the physical activity may keep them warm and thus help to prevent them from becoming hypothermic. If there is no natural shelter nearby, you will have to construct some yourself.

Innovation is the key as you must make the most of what is available. At its most simple, a shelter may well be a polythene survival bag or breathable fabric bivi-bag, but if you can also get to the leeside of a boulder or build a low wall of stones, so much the better. Indeed, if you have a casualty who cannot be moved, building a sheltering wall of stones may be your only option. If everyone in the party has a survival bag, particularly if some people have the larger double bags, there is nothing to prevent you from getting two people to share a bag.

Spare bags can then be cut along one long side and the bottom to form a large sheet of plastic which can be used to form added protection. This can be draped across the top of a boulder or a low wall, secured between two low walls, etc. Shelters of this type are best kept low as this reduces the danger of the wind getting underneath and blowing them apart. Make sure that the sheets are secured in such a way that any boulders securing them cannot be dislodged onto people sheltering. The most important consideration is protection from the wind.

Improvising shelters in winter conditions is a different ball game. Not only are conditions likely to be far more harsh, but there is also often a superb shelter-building material all around you – snow. However, here again it is better to use some form of natural shelter than to spend time and energy in digging a snow shelter. Natural snow shelters are often to be found around rocks, stone walls and trees (*see figure 45*), and many of these can be enlarged, adapted and improved by the application of a little ingenuity.

Digging a good snow shelter is not easy unless you are well practised. It can also consume a considerable

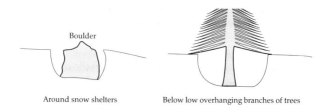

Around snow shelters       Below low overhanging branches of trees

*Figure 45: natural snow shelters*

amount of time and energy. You may feel hampered by a lack of digging equipment, although it is perfectly possible to dig a snow shelter with an ice-axe. Whatever the disadvantages, snow shelters are an extremely effective way of sheltering in winter.

There are basically two types of emergency snow shelter: those dug into banks or slopes of snow, and those formed on level ground. Regarding those in snowslopes, it is generally true to say that the steeper the slope, the easier the digging. It is also better if the entrance is a short way up the slope so that the removed material can be disposed of without too much difficulty. Start by digging a round tunnel just wider than your shoulders and begin to enlarge it once you are about 1 metre in. We are not concerned with textbook snowcaves here so much as something to keep you alive, so as long as you include the basic features, almost anything will do *(see figure 46)*.

The main considerations are that the entrance should be small and should be below the main area so that the colder air can escape. The main area itself should only be just large enough to accommodate everyone in the party, and should contain a snow bench on which to place insulating material (rope, rucksack, sleepmat, etc.) on which to sit. If the party is large, it may be advisable to dig two entrances which lead to the same main area. Ventilation is very important and should not be overlooked.

Most people will want to seal the entrance(s) in some way (with blocks of snow or rucksacks), but ventilation must be maintained both here and, in

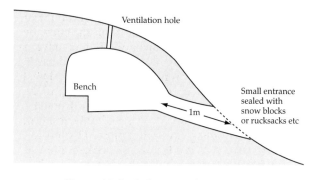

*Figure 46: basic features of a snow hole*

larger snowcaves, by forming ventilation holes in the roof or walls with the shaft of an ice axe. These ventilation holes should be checked regularly as they will easily become blocked by falling or drifting snow.

On level ground, a snow trench is probably the best option. This simply involves excavating a trench in the snow about 0.75 metres deep, piling the snow into one or preferably two walls to either side. Spare survival bags (formed into sheets as described above) can be set into these walls to form a roof. The problem with a snow trench is that there is nowhere for the cold air to escape, and unless you design it very carefully, you have a large amount of contact with the snow. Although it will provide shelter from the wind, it will be an extremely cold experience. Wherever possible, use a snow trench in conjunction with some form of natural shelter.

Whatever type of snow shelter you build, once

constructed try to keep movement in and out to a minimum and insulate yourself from the snow by whatever means come to hand. If you have a sleeping bag or bivi-bag, now is the time to use it. Once in, stay in! If you need to use a stove to heat drinks, you have a ready supply of liquid all around you, but avoid cutting snow from the inside of the main area as this will only result in everyone becoming covered in pieces of snow ice. Beware, too, creating too much condensation as this will initially freeze and subsequently drip! The most important consideration if using a stove is to make sure there is sufficient ventilation.

Mention must be made of KISU's. These are like large dome-tent flysheets. In use, the party gets into a huddle and the KISU is thrown over the top of everyone and secured by having its edges sat on! They are not widely available and come in a range of sizes from 2-man up to about 12-man. They are very effective, the people within them creating a surprising amount of heat. This will obviously be increased if a small stove is lit in the middle to boil water for a brew.

No matter what type of shelter you are in, if it is very cold you should try to keep awake. This is simply because the body's metabolism slows down during sleep and there is therefore an increased danger from hypothermia. Prepare for the night by putting on your spare clothing and insulating yourself from your surroundings, especially from the ground and any surfaces of snow or ice. If your clothing is wet and you have dry gear with you, now is the time to change. Loosen any clothing which could restrict your circulation, and untie your boot laces so as not to restrict the circulation to your feet. Throughout the long night (and it will feel like an eternity), exercise your fingers and toes, and arms and legs at regular intervals by simple clenching, hugging and stretching movements. Try to maintain morale with stories and jokes and reassure any worried people in the party. Remember that survival is predominantly an attitude. No matter how good your survival techniques, the will to live is vital.

## Improvised stretchers

Although self-evacuation is never an easy option, there may be times when it is necessary to move a casualty a short way in order to get him to a more sheltered position. It may also be possible to effect a self-rescue if an accident occurs within easy striking distance of a road. Piggy-backs and fireman's lifts are not the easiest options, especially on rough terrain. They are exhausting and upset your balance. Various techniques can be used to make the carry more comfortable for both the casualty and those people moving him.

A rucksack can be used as an improvised harness to help with a piggy-back type of carry. This is generally only possible with larger rucksacks. The basic idea is to transfer most of its contents to other rucksacks in the group, then loosen the shoulder straps to the extent that, when worn, the casualty can sit on the body of the sack (with extra padding in place if desired) with his legs through the straps (*figure 47*). This rucksack carry is only possible where the casualty has minor injuries and is able to help himself into the correct position. It will help if he sits on a boulder above the carrier, or is upslope at a steep angle. If you have a climbing rope with you, this can be used to great advantage. Although it is possible to tie a rope stretcher, this is a time consuming procedure even for experienced persons, and there are often

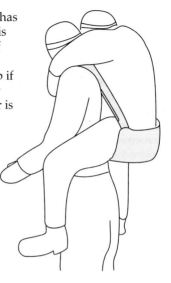

*Figure 47: rucksack carry*

better alternatives. A better way to use the rope is in some form of split rope carry. There are two basic techniques, both of which require the rope to be coiled in a mountaineer's coil *(see page 82)*.

If the coils are split down the middle, the rope can be worn like a rucksack and a form of rucksack carry can be undertaken *(figure 48)*. Some form of extra padding is desirable in this case. A less exhausting technique, perhaps, is to split the coils and share them between two people, the casualty sitting on padding on the rope between them and supporting himself by placing his arms over their shoulders. If this technique is used, the rope should be recoiled so that the coils are long enough to fit over the shoulder opposite the casualty *(figure 49)*. However, although this shares the load, it can be unstable over rough ground and there is always a danger that one person may slip or the casualty may fall off. The people carrying the casualty should be of roughly the same height.

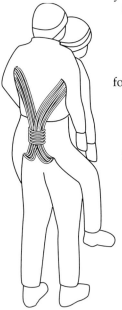

Perhaps the most useful improvised stretcher is one formed from a survival bag. In this technique, a standard polythene survival bag is used, with or without padding, carrying being facilitated by placing pebbles inside the bag then tying tape slings or climbing rope around them to form carrying handles or shoulder straps. This is quick to make and reasonably easy to carry, but it does rely on having at least four, preferably six or more people available to assist. It will also slide easily on snow.

*Figure 48: One-man split rope carry*

However, the lack of friction can be disadvantageous and the casualty can slide around with alarming ease. If using this technique, ensure that there is sufficient support for the casualty's head,

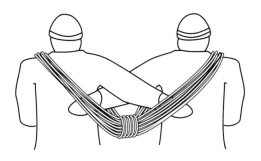

*Figure 49: two-man split rope carry*

and if carrying on a slope, ensure that he is carried head up and cannot slide off the downslope end of the bag.

## Basic search techniques

One of the problems faced when searching for a missing person is that injured people tend to go to ground. Survival instinct takes over, and they seek shelter, even if this means they are not easily visible to a search party. If involved in a search of this nature, do not make the assumption that the victim will be easily seen or will have made an effort to leave some visible clue as to his whereabouts. Sadly, this is rarely the case. The simplest search technique is that of a token search, in which you follow the intended route of the missing person. If this is not productive a sweep search is used. In its basic form, a sweep search is conducted by a group of people spread out in a long line, the distance between each person being dependent on both the nature of terrain and visibility. The line controller usually places himself somewhere near the middle of the line. Discipline within the line is very important, as is communication between members – it is too easy for it to become a collection of individuals and this will dramatically lessen the effectiveness of the search.

It is therefore important that everyone keeps their eyes on their neighbours so that as straight a line as possible is maintained. In difficult terrain where there are many places which could hide the casualty, it may be difficult to maintain line discipline as two or three people may be involved with a detailed search of a chaotic, boulder strewn area whilst others are on more open terrain. Here the distance between searchers may have to be reduced. Whatever the terrain, shouting and calling should be done at regular intervals, but there should also be definite periods of silence so that any cries for help can be heard.

In a large search, the area is usually divided into a number of sectors, each one usually being defined by a linear feature such as a stream, a long field boundary, or perhaps a ridge. Each sector is then covered by a line search. Perhaps the most important consideration in a search of this type is that the line search within any sector should be conclusive. In other words, if the casualty is there, he must be found. To be effective, searches require a fair amount of manpower. It is unlikely that you will need to use these techniques in a casual way. However, a basic knowledge of how searches are organised may be of great benefit if ever you are asked to assist with a search by a mountain rescue team. In any event, if this happens you should be well briefed by a team leader.

# 11 Further reading

Avalanche & Snow Safety,
Colin Fraser, Murray, 1978

The Avalanche Book,
Armstrong & Williams,
Fulcrum, 1992

Modern Snow & Ice
Techniques,
Bill March, Cicerone, 1973

The Backpackers' Manual,
Cameron McNeish, OIP,
1984

Wild Country Camping,
Kevin Walker, Constable,
1989

Handbook of Climbing,
Alan Fyffe & Iain Peter,
Pelham, 1990

Modern Rope Techniques,
N. Shepherd, Constable,
1990

First Aid for Hillwalkers,
Renouf & Hulse, Cicerone,
1982

Mountaineering First Aid,
Lentz, MacDonald &
Carline, The Mountaineers,
1985

Medical Handbook for
Mountaineers,
Peter Steele, Constable, 1988

Mountain Navigation
Techniques,
Kevin Walker, Constable,
1986

Mountain Hazards,
Kevin Walker, Constable,
1988

Safety on Mountains,
British Mountaineering
Council, BMC, 1991

Mountaincraft &
Leadership,
Eric Langmuir, MLTB, 1984

Mountaineering (The
Freedom of the Hills),
ed. Peters, The
Mountaineers, 1992

Mountain Weather for
Climbers,
David Unwin, Cordee, 1978

Mountain Weather, David
Pedgley,
Cicerone, 1979

The Weather Handbook,
Alan Watts, Waterline, 1994

*There are also a number of
excellent monthly publications
including High, Climber &
Hillwalker, TGO, and Trail
Walker.*